DIGGING INTO DEWEY

Diane Findlay

UpstartBooks

Fort Atkinson, Wisconsin

What would we do without public libraries? Once again I owe a huge thanks to the libraries that make it not only possible but tons of fun to do what I do. Kudos to the Children's Room staff at West Des Moines Public Library and everyone at the Waukee Public Library. They consistently go beyond the call of duty in providing skilled and enthusiastic service and support. Thanks, too, to teacher friends near and far who are so generous with the knowledge, ideas and reactions. Last, but certainly not least, my sincere appreciation goes to the gang at UpstartBooks, who are a dream and a joy to work with.

Credits:

Pages 11 (DDC Bingo and Practice with Dewey Decimal Numbers) and 116 (Decimal Dynamite Game): From *Dewey & the Decimals* by Paige Taylor and Kent & Susan Brinkmeyer. UpstartBooks, 2001.

Page 78: Story and Song from *An Alphabet of Authors* by Robin Works Davis. Highsmith Press, 1996.

Published by UpstartBooks
W5527 State Road 106
P.O. Box 800
Fort Atkinson, Wisconsin 53538-0800
1-800-448-4887

© Diane Findlay, 2005
Cover design: Debra Neu

Dewey, DDC and Dewey Decimal Classification are registered trademarks of OCLC Online Computer Library Center, Incorporated.

The paper used in this publication meets the minimum requirements of American National Standard for Information Science — Permanence of Paper for Printed Library Material. ANSI/NISO Z39.48-1992.

Table of Contents

Introduction

As the fifth- and sixth-grade creators of the ThinkQuest Web site "Do We" Really Know Dewey? observe, librarians and media specialists are always searching for "something interesting for kids about the Dewey Decimal® system." No one disputes its usefulness, even its brilliance. But how do we make it fun and exciting? Its mere mention is likely to elicit groans and yawns, rather than wild enthusiasm, from young learners. Still, library users of all ages and over much of the world rely on it to help them find what we need. A grasp of it is fundamental to any systematic pursuit of knowledge. It shouldn't be so hard to generate enthusiasm! What could be more exciting than opening the door to accessing the entire universe of human knowledge, for use by anyone who wants to explore its riches and mysteries?

As you introduce the system to elementary students, you may need to begin with an analogy that ties the concepts and content to familiar experiences. Perhaps you already have a favorite approach. If not, here's one to try:

It's Saturday, and almost time for your soccer game. But you can't find your uniform—again!—because your room looks like a tornado struck. Your things are scattered everywhere. Your mother says that you have to clean your room before you can get together
with your friends, but you don't even know where to begin! She suggests you tackle the job in steps. First, put the clothes in the closet or dresser. Then, set the books on the bookshelves. Next, return the food to the kitchen. Finally, put the toys in the toy chest or on the game shelf. Not only will that approach make the clean-up job manageable, but it will also make it easy for you to find your things next time you need them.

This scenario, or another of your choosing, can be revisited and extended as you work your way through the categories of the Dewey Decimal classification system (DDC) to keep students from getting lost in the details and help them stay grounded in the basic purpose and goals of the system. References to this analogy in the following chapters will appear in *italics*, for easy recognition and adaptation.

This book will attempt a fresh look at teaching the time-honored system to students in grades 2–6, sneaking in some fun and some library and research skills practice along the way. In these pages you'll find the ins and outs of Dewey's amazing system of classifying human knowledge, arranged in chapters to correspond with the 10 major Dewey categories. Each chapter offers an introduction to its hundred range, what it includes and why, the tens subcategories, interesting related print and nonprint resources and a sampling of games and activities to familiarize students with the subject matter being discussed and how to access it. Out of each, you should be able to craft stand-alone library lessons appropriate to your particular situation and students.

Because libraries are at different levels of transition from card to electronic catalogs, because children have widely varying exposure to and skills with computers and because serious catalog searches require a sophistication beyond the scope of this book, you will not find computer catalog activities in each chapter. Instead, I encourage you to adapt ideas to your particular circumstances. Some examples of computer activities show up in the Exploring the DDC System chapter, along with other activities and exercises that can be used with study of any of the hundreds categories in the DDC.

All titles in the chapter bibliographies are in print or readily available in libraries. They were chosen for the best combination of quality, balance and usefulness in exploring the subject content of their chapters. I hope you will add your own favorites and adapt the activities to suit your needs.

A few general resources might be useful throughout your exploration of the DDC and the world of knowledge it seeks to unlock. The Web site mentioned at the beginning of this introduction is fun and surprisingly informative, offering not just whimsical stories, quizzes and puzzles, but basic organizing principles of the system and tricks for navigating it effectively. Look for it at **library.thinkquest.org/5002,** or

visit **www.thinkquest.org** and search by site title ("Do We" Really Know Dewey?). Another Web site, OCLC's Take a Tour of the DDC (**www.oclc.org/dewey/resources/tour),** offers an excellent and interesting, if quite detailed, "movie version" look at the structure and function of the system which older students might explore a section at a time. Related pages tell Dewey's story and let students test their knowledge with quizzes. Another Web site, The Dewey Decimal System (**www.cte.jhu.edu/techacad emy/web/2000/foster/index.htm),** involves students in a challenge with steps to follow and a culminating project, and serves as an umbrella site for several other sites mentioned in this book. And KidsClick! Web Search **(sunsite. berkeley.edu/KidsClick!/dewey.html)** lets kids browse for interesting Web sites by Dewey number. Allan Fowler's *The Dewey Decimal System,* from the Children's Press True Books series is a good introduction at the easy reader level. And *Dewey & the Decimals,* by Paige Taylor and Kent & Susan Brinkmeyer (also available from Upstart Books), is full of clever, fun games and activities, a few of which are borrowed or adapted in the following chapters. The latter title includes suggestions for a bulletin board display about the DDC that changes as you work through the system, and how to involve students in creating and maintaining it. Upstart also carries an attractive set of posters, each featuring one of the 100s categories. Coordinating banner and bookmarks summarize the system by listing all of the 100s categories.

Exploring the Dewey Decimal Classification System

Use these ideas to help you introduce concepts and practice skills related to using the DDC. Most of the activities can be used with any one or more of the hundreds categories covered in the following chapters.

Basic Concepts to Present in Lecture/Demonstration/Discussion Mode

- **Fiction and Nonfiction, Part I.** Explain to students that one of the first, most general ways to classify books and other library materials is to decide if they are fiction or nonfiction. The "Do We" Really Know Dewey? Web site mentioned in the Introduction offers an easy, if superficial, trick for remembering the distinction: You can "only say 'NO' once: Fiction=Not true, Nonfiction=True." Made-up stories are fiction. Books that give factual information, state research-based opinions or tell the truth about a subject are nonfiction. Show students clear examples of each from your collection and ask them to suggest other books they know as examples of fiction or nonfiction. Explain that when you're just looking for something fun to read, you can browse the fiction shelves and see what catches your eye. Maybe you have a favorite author, and want to read more of what he or she has written. So the fiction shelves are arranged in alphabetical order by the author's last name with all the books by the same author together. But if you want to learn the facts about a particular subject, it doesn't matter who wrote the book as much as that the book talks about the subject you're investigating. That's where the DDC comes in. Explain that the DDC is mainly designed to organize nonfiction materials that are used more for study and learning than for simple entertainment. This leads into the introductory discussion of the DDC found in the 000s chapter on page 15.

- **Fiction and Nonfiction, Part II.** At some point in your study, your students may ask questions about, or be ready for more complete and sophisticated explanations of, the distinction between fiction and nonfiction.

Be prepared to explain that it isn't always obvious whether a particular item should go on the fiction or nonfiction shelves. Give examples, like these:

- **Historical Fiction.** Stories based on well-researched, historical events have a lot of "nonfiction content" in them. But if the author has made up a lot of the story, changed the characters, had them say words they didn't really say, etc., so that we can't be sure which parts are true and which are made up, it will probably be classified as fiction.

- **Collections of Favorite Children's Stories.** Folktales, fairy tales, nursery rhymes, etc., are clearly made-up stories. But are they used just for fun and entertainment, or do they teach us things about the beliefs and customs of the people and societies they came from? Are they written in more than one language or in a language other than English, to help us study languages? Or are they so universal and timeless in their themes and expressions of human experience that we might study them to understand how groups of people think and act over time? If so, they might be classified as nonfiction.

- **Poems, Plays, Riddles and Jokes.** Often, these styles of writing are entirely made up in their content. But because of their forms we may use them differently than we use prose fiction. We might be looking for jokes to tell in a speech, poems to add to a love letter or scenes from plays to act out for a talent contest. So the form of the writing becomes more important than the creative, make-believe content, and it helps us to group them together by type on the nonfiction shelves.

- **Holiday Books.** Many books in a library's holidays collection are probably fiction. But again, how are they used? Readers are more likely to want them, along with other titles about a particular holiday, during that holiday season. So

it's more helpful to put all the Halloween books together, rather than scatter them throughout the collection by author name or specific subject matter (cooking, crafts, history, etc.).

Explain that the only way to be sure to find what you want is to start with the library's catalog, using the title, author name or subject you're looking for. The catalog will direct you to appropriate items on the shelves.

- **Call Numbers.** Early on in your orientation to the DDC, you'll need to explain about and demonstrate call numbers and their location on the items in your collection. After discussing the distinction between fiction and nonfiction, show students several items and point out the spine labels with call numbers. Explain that the letters and numbers written on the labels tell us exactly where the items belong on the library shelves. They're like your street address, which tells people exactly where to find you. Look at the ends of the book stacks. They probably have signs with letters (in the fiction section) or numbers (in the nonfiction Dewey section) on them. They lead you from the call numbers you found in the catalog to the items on the shelves, just like street signs on the corners lead people from your address to your house. Pass around examples of items with spine labels and explain how your media center shows location on the labels. For example, whether your children's fiction is designated "F," "JF" or "Fic," it probably has no numbers in the top line. Explain what the letters, including the letters in the second line that indicate the author's name, mean in the context of your collection. By contrast, whether your media center puts a "J" in front of the Dewey number or not, a three-digit (or longer) number on the top line of the label clearly identifies it as nonfiction and indicates its place in the numerically-ordered nonfiction shelves. Point out that, like fiction call numbers, nonfiction call numbers will usually indicate the author's name on the last line. As long as the readers who look for books, and the staff members who put them back after they're used, read the call numbers carefully, each item will always be easy to find in its one-and-only "right" place in the collection. If your library has a noncirculating reference collection, designated with an "R" at the beginning, point that out along with any other special designations used on call numbers.

- **Organizing Principle #1: Grouping Like Things Together.** The DDC is organized around two fairly simple ideas or principles. The first is to group similar items together. For example, all of the books about learning to draw will be found together on the shelves in the 740s, so once you find the Dewey number for your subject, you'll only have to look in one place for the items you want. Of course, it's not always that simple, as we'll learn. But Dewey follows that basic, logical, efficient principle as much as possible. When presenting this principle, you might take students to the shelves and show them several clusters of materials grouped together based on their subject-related Dewey numbers.

- **Organizing Principle #2: General to Specific.** The second basic principle Dewey used in designing his classification system was to move from the broad and general to the narrow and specific. So you'll find Generalities (reference works like encyclopedias and newspapers that address every subject under the sun!) at the very beginning of the system, in the 000s, followed by hundreds categories that address defined and limited, if still rather broad, subject areas. And within each hundreds category, you'll find "General Works" at the very beginning (General Works about Religion in the 200s, General Works about Technology in the 600s, etc.) before the tens groups break the subjects down further. In turn, within each tens group, the ones column is used to get even more specific. For

example, the 300s cover the social sciences. The 390s look more narrowly at social customs and folklore. And items in 391 focus specifically on clothing and costumes. Use an example from your own collection, so you can point to specific titles that demonstrate this principle. This is called a hierarchical system, and it's the reason why every Dewey number has at least three digits to it, in order to indicate where exactly it fits in the context of its ones, tens and hundreds places.

- **General to Specific to VERY Specific!** Later in your study, when students have grasped the basic concepts and operating principles of the system, you can introduce the additional specificity provided by decimal numbers. A good time to do this is when you get to the 500s, for two reasons. You're halfway through the system, so students should be getting familiar and comfortable with how it all works, and starting to get a feel for the whole range of ideas being organized and, therefore, the need for very specific distinctions within categories and groups. And the 500s include math, which makes it easy to enlist the help of math teachers in exploring and explaining decimals. Here's what's important for students to know: 1) There's no limit to the number of digits that can be added past the decimal point, in order to define more and more specific distinctions among similar subjects. Librarians who refine and apply the DDC are constantly adding and recombining decimal numbers to reflect new developments and very specific detail within subject areas. 2) The longer the number, the more specific the topic covered in the material. Again, show examples from your collection and analyze them on the board to demonstrate the principle, as follows:

Dewey # 796.342
  700s Fine Arts and Recreation
    790s Recreation and Performing Art
      796 Athletic or outdoor sports and games
        796.3 Ball games

Activities to Practice Skills and Master the DDC

- **Find it by Number!** Familiarize students with the physical location of the Dewey-numbered nonfiction in the media center and get them started reading and finding call numbers. Point out that items are shelved from left to right, and from top to bottom on each shelf section, just like words are ordered on a page. Place bright-colored paper place markers, with Dewey numbers clearly written on them, at appropriate spots in the nonfiction shelves and have individual students or small teams find them as assigned. For younger grades, you might mark the divisions between the hundreds categories and assign teams of two to three students to find "where the numbers starting with 0 (1, 2, etc.) begin." For older grades, you might mark specific three-digit call numbers (no decimals at first), and assign individuals or teams corresponding numbers to locate. Give each student or team an index card with their assigned number ("000," "398," etc.). Students will turn in their matching cards and shelf markers—perhaps trading markers for small prizes.

- **Find it by Subject! Part I** Assign students specific one or two-word subject headings that fall into the hundreds category you are studying. For example, if you are exploring the 500s, you might give students subject headings like "Mars" or "Desert Animals." Have them search your collection for one or more titles that address their subject. Try having students look for appropriate titles by browsing the hundreds area on the shelves first. Then have them use the library catalog to identify titles and the Dewey call numbers to find on the shelves. This will demonstrate the time and effort saved by working from the catalog and using Dewey call numbers. Students will write down the titles, authors and call numbers of the titles they find, to show they completed the exercise.

- **Find it by Subject! Part II** Build on the previous exercise for older students, as you get further along in studying the system, by assigning trickier subject headings that might be covered in two or more distinct parts of the DDC. For example, titles about different aspects of "Humor" might show up in 398, in the comedy section of the 790s or in the 810s or 820s. Likewise, different aspects of business might be found in the 380s or 650s. After completing the exercise, discuss reasons why material on the same general subject might be classified in different parts of the DDC, depending on what aspect of the subject is most important in the specific item. Remind students that using the catalog is the only way to be sure they've found everything the library has to offer on their subject.

- **Discussion: What Goes Here?** After introducing a particular hundreds category and the tens groupings within it, show books or other materials that fit in that category. Then ask students to suggest titles of books they might write that would be classified in that category, and which tens category they fit best. Students might suggest such things as "My Dad's a Reporter" in the 070s, "My Dream Journal" in the 150s, "Learning about Hinduism" in the 290s," "How to Win an Election" in the 320s, "My Life as an Adjective" in the 420s, "101 Math Tricks" in the 510s, "The Best Babysitter's Guidebook" in the 640s, "Collecting Postage Stamps" in the 760s, "Terrifying Tongue Twisters" in the 810s or "A History of Slavery" in the 900s.

- **Numbers Scramble.** This timed contest reinforces the concept of numbered subject categories in the DDC and gives practice in numerical order. Before class, decide how many teams you'll use. Pull items from the shelves and create stacks containing an equal number of books for each team. For younger students, you might choose stacks of 8–10 books, each from a different Dewey hundreds category and starting with a different number from 0–9. For older students, you might stay within a hundreds category and pull 8–10 books from different tens groups. Divide students into teams. Give each team one of the stacks, covered with a large piece of cloth or paper. Tell the teams that their task is to arrange their books in order, according to the first digit (or two digits) in their Dewey call numbers. As soon as a team finishes, they should raise their hands. Say "Go!" to start. As the teams raise their hands, keep track of the order in which they finish—teams could be identified by different colored cloth or paper covers for their stacks of books. When all teams are done, check their work in the order in which they finish. The team that correctly completes the task first wins.

- **Find it Fast!** Divide the class into three to four teams. Give each team a set of cards (face down) equal to the number of students on the team. Each card should have a different tens group of the hundreds group you are studying written on it (e.g., 200, 230, 290). Be sure you have enough titles on your shelves clearly labeled in each grouping you identify. When you say "Go," teams should deal out their cards, turn them over, go to the shelves and collect an item that fits in their Dewey tens number, return to the lesson area and arrange themselves in numerical order with appropriate materials held up in front of them. The first team to correctly complete the task is the winner.

- **DDC Bingo.** The sample on page 12 can be used with the 000s, and serve as a model for making the game for any of the hundreds categories. Make a copy of the game board and subject squares on page 12 for each student. Pass out copies, scissors, glue and 10 markers (buttons, pennies or colored bits of paper to cover game board squares as you play) to each student. Point out that subjects and their Dewey numbers form a column directly below their corresponding tens group above, e.g., "Museum Management (069)" and "Directory of kids' fan clubs (060)" are in the column below "General Organizations & Museums (060s)." Have students cut apart the nine columns of printed subject squares. They will each choose one subject square from each tens group column to cut out and glue onto the blank space directly below the appropriate tens group title on the game board. This will make each student's bingo card individual. Cut apart the 36 printed subject squares from a separate copy and place them in a container. Have students take turns picking a subject square out of the container and reading it aloud. Students who have the matching subject square on their bingo card will cover it with a marker. The first student to cover all 10 game board squares shouts "Bingo!" and wins the game.

- **Practice with Dewey Decimal Numbers.** Use the reproducible worksheet on page 13 to give students practice placing possible Dewey decimal numbers in proper order. The worksheet includes three skill levels. You might assign a particular skill level, or challenge students to complete as many columns as they can based on their grasp of decimal ordering. You could create similar lists for other hundreds categories.

Tens Groups Game Board

Unexplained Phenomena, Computers and Internet 000s	Bibliography 010s	Libraries and Information Science 020s	General Encyclopedias and Atlases 030s	Unassigned 040s	General Interest Magazines 050s	General Organizations and Museums 060s	News Media, Journalism Publishing 070s	General Collections 080s	Manuscripts and Rare Books 090s
				FREE					

DEWEY DECIMAL CLASSIFICATION SYSTEM BINGO

—— GAME BOARD ——

Game Board Squares

World of UFOs 001	List of free stuff for kids 011	Dewey Decimal System 025	General Encyclopedias In English 031	Reader's Guide to Periodical Literature 051	Museum management 069	Careers in journalism 070	Quotes on life from children 081	Teaching banned books 098
History of books 002	Best books for kids 011	Being a librarian 020	Books of World Records 031	American current events magazines 051	Guide to the Smithsonian Institute 069	First American newspaper 071	Interviews with fascinating people 082	Collecting rare books 090
Computer programming 005	Index to fairy tales 016	The Library of Congress 027	Encyclopedia in Spanish 036	German language magazines 053	Directory of kids' fan clubs 060	Publishing a book 070	Essays on life 081	Early printed books 094
The Loch Ness Monster 000	List of fiction sequels 016	Using libraries 025	World almanac 031	Children's magazines in Arabic 059	Americana Hall of Fame 069	Famous journalists 070	Famous quotations in French 084	Miniature books 099

—— MARKERS ——

Practice with Decimals

Below are lists of decimal numbers, which need to be placed in order, starting with the lowest number at the top. Choose your skill level and then write the decimals in their correct order (1–10) in the blanks to the right of each series.

Skill Level 1	Skill Level 2	Skill Level 3
429. 1 _____	711.11 _____	928.001 _____
533.9 _____	711.01 _____	928.0101 _____
333.5 _____	701.11 _____	928.101 _____
849.4 _____	700.01 _____	928.19 _____
952.1 _____	700.11 _____	928.023 _____
651.8 _____	710.11 _____	928.03 _____
241.2 _____	710.01 _____	928.031 _____
182.5 _____	710.07 _____	928.0031 _____
041.3 _____	710.77 _____	928.213 _____
711.1 _____	717.01 _____	928.312 _____

000s: Generalities

The major organizing principles of the Dewey Decimal classification system are 1) grouping related subjects together and 2) moving from the general to the specific. Each hundreds category operates on these principles. The 000s—Generalities—uniquely demonstrates the second principle, starting off the system with materials that broadly address general knowledge, rather than limiting themselves to a particular discipline or branch of knowledge. Back to our disorderly room scenario:

About 125 years ago, a man named Melvil Dewey faced a similar—but much bigger—challenge to the messy room problem we talked about earlier. He wanted to learn about everything in the world! He knew there were many ways to learn about all different subjects through books, magazines and newspapers. But how would he make his way through all of the information about everything that people think and know about? Where should he start? How could he help other people who wanted to learn to organize the whole world of knowledge and ideas into a manageable system, so they could find the information they wanted when they wanted it? This was a huge task! This makes your messy room look like a snap!

Well, maybe Dewey knew the mother from our example, because he took a similar approach. He thought about the whole world of information, and

divided it up into categories of ideas that were related to each other—sort of like organizing your things into clothes, books, toys, etc. He grouped together similar subjects and assigned them numbers. He started by dividing all of human knowledge into ten major groups, which became the hundreds categories of the Dewey Decimal classification system. For example, he put all the materials about science and math in the 500s, and everything about history and geography in the 900s. (Show the whole system of 100s categories here.) Then, because each of these categories still had so many different ideas in it, he divided each one into smaller groups, which became the tens groupings. You use the same idea, in organizing your room, if you put all your school clothes in one part of your closet, your play clothes in another and your underwear and socks in a dresser drawer. So all the materials on math fall into the 510s, while those that talk about the lives of wild animals are in the 590s.

Dewey thought this was a good system, and libraries all over the world agreed and still use it today. The appropriate numbers from Dewey's system are put on books or other materials, which are stored together by number so you can find them easily. But right away, Dewey ran into some problems. Think about this: What would you do with that silly hat your Aunt Mavis gave you for your birthday, with the propeller on top and that also flies like a Frisbee? Is it clothing or a toy? Does it belong in the dresser or in the toy chest (or, possibly, the wastebasket)? Does your stuffed bear/sleepover bag go on your bed with the stuffed animals or in your closet with your backpack and suitcase? This sort of dilemma is exactly why Dewey started out his system with the 000s (say "zero hundreds") for "Generalities." This is where you'll find materials that don't fit in a single subject category because they deal with many different subjects at once. Things like encyclopedias and atlases, general interest magazines and newspapers, libraries and museums. Also in this hundreds group are computers, which help us find information on anything you can think of. And there's a place for "unexplained phenomena" like the Loch Ness Monster and Bigfoot because, let's be honest, Dewey couldn't figure out where else to put them!

These are the tens groups in the 000s category:

- 000s: Unexplained Phenomena, Computers and the Internet

- 010s: Bibliography (general lists of materials)

- 020s: Libraries and Information Science (Including the Dewey Decimal classification system!)

- 030s: General Encyclopedias

- 040s: (Unassigned)

- 050s: General Interest Magazines

- 060s: General Organizations and Museums

- 070s: News Media, Journalism and Publishing

- 080s: General Collections

- 090s: Manuscripts and Rare Books

Resources on the 000s

Here are some print and nonprint resources to help you explain and explore the 000s category of the DDC. They, along with other titles from your collection, could be placed on display or built into your lesson plans.

Print Resources

- ***Beastly Tales: Yeti, Bigfoot and the Loch Ness Monster*** by Malcolm Yorke. DK Publishing, 1998. 2–4. This Eyewitness Readers series title shares accounts of personal encounters with these mysterious creatures along with photos and drawings, public response and attempts to prove or disprove their existence. A quick, easy, interesting read.

- ***The Boggart and the Monster*** by Susan Cooper. Simon & Schuster, 1998. 3–6. Cooper works her magic in another adventure featuring Emily and Jessup Volnik, Tommy Cameron and the Boggart of Castle Keep. When the Jessups visit the castle they are caught up in a potentially disastrous search for the Loch Ness Monster, with surprising and satisfying results.

- ***Encyclopedia Brown and the Case of the Slippery Salamander*** by Donald J. Sobol. Bantam Doubleday Dell, 2000. 3–5. The 10-year-old wunderkind is back, using his encyclopedic knowledge of obscure facts to catch criminals. Ten clever scenarios challenge the reader to keep up with the spunky walking reference book as he solves mysteries by applying general knowledge and basic logic.

- ***The Furry News: How to Make a Newspaper*** by Loreen Leedy. Holiday House, 1996. 2–4. Big Bear decides that the city newspaper slights his animal neighborhood and recruits local critters to create their own paper. They, and we, learn about publishing, news reporting, feature articles, production, circulation and advertising. A

final spread summarizes a simple process for making your own school or neighborhood newspaper.

- ***The House of Wisdom*** by Florence Parry Heide and Judith Heide Gilliland, illustrated by Mary Grandpré. DK Publishing, 1999. 2–6. This lyrical picture book tells the true story of a wondrous library and center of learning that existed in Iraq in the ninth century. It celebrates the value of knowledge and culture, and is particularly timely in light of the very different picture of Iraq that we see today. Grandpré's illustrations may entice young readers familiar with her drawings in the Harry Potter books.

- ***How a Book is Published*** by Bobbie Kalman. Crabtree Publishing Company, 1995. 2–4. This well-designed little book presents the world of writing and publishing in a nutshell. An excellent balance of appealing illustration and clear text makes the complex process accessible even to younger students.

- ***The Inside-Outside Book of Libraries*** by Julie Cummins, illustrated by Roxie Munro. Penguin Putnam, 1996. 2–4. The overbalance of attractive, content-rich illustrations to text makes this introduction to a dozen very diverse libraries (including a prison library, the Andrew Heiskell Library for the Blind and Physically Handicapped and bookmobiles) inviting and effective. It conveys a clear message: Libraries come in all shapes and sizes to help people learn and do.

- ***Internet for Kids*** by Ted Pedersen and Francis Moss. Penguin Putnam, 1997. 4–6. Welcome to Cyberspace Academy! Young readers become cadets under the instruction of CyberSarg, who leads them through Internet vocabulary, search strategies, protocol, safety and much more. A visually appealing, information-packed guide for kids and parents who want to be successful "Internauts."

- **A Kid's Guide to the Smithsonian** by Ann Phillips Bay. The Smithsonian Institution Press, 1996. 4–6. This bright, inviting guide introduces the concept of museums, the history of the Smithsonian and the amazing and varied holdings of its sixteen museums, concentrating on the Castle, the National Air and Space Museum, the National Museum of American History and the National Museum of Natural History. Hybrid illustrations—part photograph and part drawings by Steven Rotblatt, add color and character.

- **McBroom's Almanac** by Sid Fleischman, illustrated by Walter Lorraine. Little, Brown and Company, 1984. 3–6. If students don't already know Josh McBroom, this is a perfect introduction. His hilarious version of the classic almanac features his ten children, one-acre farm and crotchety neighbor in anecdotes, agricultural tips, pithy sayings, nature lore, household hints, weather forecasts and general advice. Delightful silliness.

- **Mrs. Brown on Exhibit: And Other Museum Poems** by Susan Katz, illustrated by R. W. Alley. Simon & Schuster, 2002. 2–5. Ms. Frizzle, of The Magic School Bus fame, has a kindred soul in Mrs. Brown, whose own brand of enthusiasm and zaniness runs toward museums. Her class explores in poetry a wide range of museums, coming face-to-face with mummies, dinosaurs, fine art, bugs, a giant heart, weather phenomena and more. A list of quirky museums all over the country demonstrates their amazing range. Great fun.

- **The Serial Sneak Thief** by E. W. Hildick. Marshall Cavendish, 1997. 4–6. Felicity Snell, librarian extraordinaire, is at it again!

A mystery contest designed to involve children in the library takes on a new level of excitement when a real mystery—involving an elusive rare materials thief—develops. Will the kids on the "Watchdog Squad" save the day?

- **Time for Kids Almanac 2004** with Information Please, edited by Beth Rowen. Time Inc., 2003. 3–6. This busy, colorful hodgepodge of wide-ranging information invites sampling, while a detailed table of contents and index add to research value.

Nonprint Resources

- **World Book Encyclopedia 2004 Edition.** World Book, Inc., 2003 (Interactive CD). 3+. In addition to standard encyclopedia articles and graphics on thousands of topics, this software version offers videos, audio clips and Web links. An exclusive feature called "Surf the Ages" presents made-up but research-based "Web sites" that offer information on important periods of history as though created in that time and place.

Web Resources

- **About**
  www.about.com

- **Ask Jeeves for Kids**
  www.ajkids.com

- **Kidspace @ The Internet Public Library**
  www.ipl.org/div/kidspace

- **Lycos Kids**
  www.lycos.com
  Click on the "Kids" link.

- **Yahooligans**
  www.yahooligans.com

Activities for the 000s

Use these activities in the media center or classroom, as parts of a single-period library lesson or in cooperation with classroom teachers. The ideas address standards across the curriculum.

- **Story.** Read aloud *The House of Wisdom* to get a feel for the breadth of human knowledge that Dewey (later) tried to make accessible, and for the joy of learning. This book is particularly interesting for its current events relevance. At a time when all most students know about Iraq relates to war and political chaos, it tells a positive story about learning and culture in Baghdad's history. It could stimulate discussion, to be pursued as time allows, about how countries can change over time and about the connection between a country's social and political well-being and the value it places on knowledge and education.

- **Dewey Decimal Classification System Word Search.** Have students fill in the blanks and then locate the words related to the DDC and Generalities, using the reproducible word search on page 21. **Answers:** 1. Dewey, 2. nonfiction, 3. Classification, 4. together, 5. general, 6. ten, 7. generalities, 8. find, 9. call, 10. music.

- **Song.** Combine this song with a chart showing the hundreds and tens groupings of the DDC to summarize your introduction of the system. Sing it to the tune of "Old McDonald." Have students make up additional verses to demonstrate their understanding.

  Melvil Dewey had a plan,
  Thought you'd like to know,
  To put all knowledge in our hands,
  Just to help us know.

  He put science here *(Point to 500s on chart)*.
  And music there *(Point to 780s)*.
  History *(Point to 900s)*, philosophy *(Point to 100s)*.

Writing *(Point to 800s)* and technology *(Point to 600s)*.

Melvil Dewey had a plan—
He still helps us know.

- **"E" is for Encyclopedia and Everything!** This activity offers practice in alphabetical order and demonstrates the idea of "general information" found in an encyclopedia. Choose a comprehensive children's encyclopedia, with lots of pictures, from your 000s collection. Then hand out cards with letters of the alphabet on them. Depending on how much time you want to spend, you might give each student a card or choose five to eight students to participate as a demonstration. For younger students, cards should have only a single letter. For older students, you might use a narrower but deeper range of letters. For example, in a fifth grade class, you might use five cards reading "FA," "FR," "FO," "FI" and "FL." Then proceed with the steps below.

  - Have students line up in alphabetical order based on the letters on their cards.

  - Have each student suggest a topic that begins with his or her letter(s) and that might be covered in the encyclopedia.

  - Look up the suggested topic. If it is covered, show the article to the class. If not, have the student try again until he or she comes up with a topic that corresponds to an entry in the encyclopedia.

  - Summarize that encyclopedias are classified in "generalities" because they deal with many different subjects at once, and review other materials that are found in the 000s for the same reason.

- **General Knowledge Bingo.** Use the reproducible game sheet on page 22 to give students practice finding general information in resources from your media center's 000s collection. You can adjust the challenge level by assigning it to individuals or teams and by requiring students to complete either a vertical, horizontal or diagonal row or the entire sheet to "win."

- **Extra Credit Book Review.** Work with classroom teachers to offer students an option to earn extra credit by reading a fiction book related to the Dewey 000s subjects and turning in a written book review and/or illustration. Results could be displayed in the media center. Suggest *The Boggart and the Monster*, any Encyclopedia Brown title, *The Serial Sneak Thief* or other Felicity Snell novels, *McBroom's Almanac* or other titles of your choosing.

- **Poetry Learning Center.** This could be done in the media center or classroom. Start by reading or reviewing *Mrs. Brown on Exhibit* and *The Inside-Outside Book of Libraries*. Then place the books at a learning center and invite students to use *Mrs. Brown on Exhibit* as a model to create their own poems about exploring the contents of museums or libraries. Their poems could be written or recorded on cassettes, and shared as part of a media center display on the Dewey 000s.

- **Math Tie-in: Set Theory.** Suggest to teachers that they offer the Dewey Decimal classification system as a good example of sets and subsets when they discuss set theory in math class.

- **Science Tie-in: Scientific Method.** Suggest to teachers that they explore the evidence supporting various theories about Loch Ness Monster, Bigfoot, crop circles or other unexplained phenomena from the 000s when they introduce the concept of scientific investigation in class. Theories about various phenomena could be separately assigned to individual students or small groups to review and evaluate as a research exercise as well.

- **Language Arts/Visual Arts Tie-in: School Newspaper.** Work with classroom teachers to have the class create an issue of a school newspaper, based on the sample and instructions in *The Furry News: How to Make a Newspaper*. Cover a wide range of subjects, in keeping with the concept of Generalities. Display and distribute the newspaper in the media center.

Dewey Decimal Classification System Word Search

Fill in the blanks or circle the correct answer in the following sentences. Then look for your answers on the word search grid below. Words might appear forward or backwards, across, up and down or diagonally on the grid.

1. Melvil _ _ _ _ _ created a system we still use to organize library collections.

2. Is this system most often used to classify fiction or nonfiction materials? _ _ _ _ _ _ _ _ _ _

3. The abbreviation "DDC" stands for Dewey Decimal _ _ _ _ _ _ _ _ _ _ _ _ _ _ .

4. One of the main ideas of the DDC is to store materials on related subjects _ _ _ _ _ _ _ _ .

5. Another main idea of the DDC is to start with broad, _ _ _ _ _ _ _ subjects and move to more specific subjects.

6. Dewey divided all knowledge into _ _ _ main categories.

7. The first hundreds category of the DDC, the 000s, covers _ _ _ _ _ _ _ _ _ _ _ _ _ .

8. The DDC is designed to help us _ _ _ _ the information we need on any subject.

9. You'll find a book's DDC classification as part of the _ _ _ _ number on the book's spine.

10. Which of the following topics does not belong in the DDC 000s category?

    • computers   • music   • museums   • Bigfoot

```
C  V  L  I  C  A  E  D  N  N  H  D  G  I  S
J  L  B  A  G  A  L  H  O  J  M  K  E  K  E
V  H  A  G  R  E  L  N  H  T  N  S  N  X  Q
E  F  O  S  W  E  F  L  X  E  R  V  E  M  E
P  Q  O  T  S  I  N  U  U  Y  A  R  S  P
J  E  H  F  C  I  R  E  C  B  N  C  A  C  T
T  C  I  T  J  W  F  T  G  P  F  R  L  C  U
J  F  I  N  D  L  T  I  K  Z  N  C  I  Y  F
Q  O  L  Y  C  Y  J  L  C  R  V  S  T  P  R
N  R  E  H  T  E  G  O  T  A  U  M  I  D  U
B  T  R  M  J  W  X  X  U  M  T  L  E  V  C
Q  T  Y  J  N  E  S  B  E  Y  C  I  S  Y  T
Q  E  V  S  Y  D  B  Z  M  H  H  T  O  X  Z
P  N  A  S  W  C  A  P  Z  U  E  K  U  N  X
N  N  G  I  Z  L  Y  I  S  D  T  D  E  P  C
```

General Knowledge Bingo Game

Use Dewey Decimal Classification 000s resources in your classroom or media center to answer the questions in the bingo squares below.

The capital city of Syria is _____ .	How many players make up a hockey team? _____	How old was Pablo Picasso when he died? _____	Who was our twelfth president? _____	Botany is the scientific study of _____ .
Rock music began in what country? _____	What is the main language spoken in Brazil? _____	Who created Mickey Mouse? _____	What religion did Muhammad found? _____	What do the letters "ESP" stand for? _____
Where is Mt. Vesuvius located? _____	Name a play written by William Shakespeare. _____	FREE	Who discovered the North Pole? _____	What chemical element is abbreviated "Ti"? _____
Who invented the game of baseball? _____	Who is the oldest known living person? _____	How old do you have to be to become president of the United States? _____	What medical specialty studies diseases in children? _____	What does the computer term ISP stand for? _____
What is your state's official state flower? _____	How much of the earth is covered by water? _____	What is the world's tallest building? _____	What time did the sun rise where you live on January 10 of this year? _____	What did Thor control, according to Norse myths? _____

100s: Philosophy & Psychology: Thinking About Ourselves

Mr. Dewey must have chosen what to include in the next hundreds category, the 100s, based again on that second organizing principle—of moving from the general to the specific. In the 000s we looked at information sources outside ourselves that address many different subjects. In the 100s, Philosophy and Psychology, we look inside ourselves for the ways we think and the questions we ask about ourselves and everything around us. We talk about great thinkers and the pursuit of wisdom. We examine how our minds work and ask the biggest, most puzzling and far-reaching questions we can imagine. How do we think? What does it mean to be human? How do people relate to the universe? What is right and what is wrong? Are there mysterious powers of the human mind that we don't understand? While we don't have clear answers to these big questions and probably never will, pondering them seems natural to us as people. As the French philosopher Descartes expressed it, "I think, therefore I am."

Note that the first tens group, listed on page 24, covers "General Works about Philosophy and Psychology." This is another example, this time within a hundreds category, of moving from the general to the specific. General works provide an overview or summary of many aspects of the overall subject area and come first in the system. Narrower and more specific aspects of the overall subject follow in later tens groups. You'll see this pattern repeated in each remaining hundreds category.

In terms of our messy room scenario, we might think of it this way. In the 000s, we dealt with things that had different uses and could fit in different groups (the hat that is also a toy, the overnight bag that is also a stuffed animal). In the 100s, we stop and look at our organizing process. What is the real purpose and use of each item? How do we think about it, and how are we most likely to use it and remember it? What does it mean to us? For example, while the baseball signed by Sammy Sosa and given to you by your favorite uncle is "just a toy," it's more important to you than the sports equipment you play with. You decide to keep it in a display case with other treasures—not because of what it is, but because of how you think of it and what it represents to you. Or consider your good luck penny. It's a coin, so it could go in your piggy bank. It's on a chain, so you might keep it in your jewelry box. But because of its special meaning for you, you choose to wear it or keep it with you in your pocket. This kind of examination of the deeper meaning of things and how we feel about them is what the Dewey 100s category is all about.

These are the tens groups in the 100s category:

- 100s: General Works on Philosophy and Psychology

- 110s: Metaphysics (What is real and what does it mean to exist?)

- 120s: Epistemology, Causation and Humankind (The study of knowledge and what it means to be human.)

- 130s: Parapsychology (The study of unexplained powers of the mind.)

- 140s: Philosophical Schools and Doctrines (Groups, organizations and methods involved in pursuing wisdom.)

- 150s: Psychology (The study of the mind, emotions and behavior.)

- 160s: Logic (The study of the basic principles of reasoning.)

- 170s: Ethics (The study of right and wrong.)

- 180s: Ancient, Medieval and Eastern Philosophy

- 190s: Modern Western Philosophy

Resources on the 100s

Here are some print and nonprint resources to help you explain and explore the 100s category of the DDC. They, along with other titles from your collection, could be placed on display or built into your lesson plans.

Print Resources

- **Being Your Best: Character Building for Kids 7–10** by Barbara A. Lewis. Free Spirit Publishing, 1999. 4–6. This friendly, approachable book helps children look at "what's inside." It introduces the idea of character and character traits, helps kids assess their own strengths and weaknesses and explores ten qualities of character—a sort of "Personal Ethics 101" for children.

- **The Boy Who Could Fly Without a Motor** by Theodore Taylor. Harcourt, 2002. 3–6. Nine-year-old Jon lives on a tiny island with his parents, the lighthouse keepers. Desperately lonely, he longs to escape his isolation by flying. His fervent wishes conjure a mysterious figure, who shares with him the secret mental power of unaided flight. But Jon soon learns that extraordinary gifts can cause extraordinary problems.

- **Confucius: The Golden Rule** by Russell Freedman, illustrated by Frederic Clement. Scholastic, 2000. 3–6. This beautifully illustrated biography by award-winner Freedman balances fact and fiction, carefully acknowledging the dearth of verifiable information about the philosopher's life while appreciating the enduring, legendary wisdom attributed to him. A great example of how relevant "ancient Eastern philosophy" is to us today.

- **Elbert's Bad Word** by Audrey Wood and Don Wood. Harcourt, 1996. 2–6. When a croquet mallet falls on Elbert's toe the ugly bad word that has sneaked into his mouth springs out, to everyone's dismay! It takes a kind gardener-wizard to "cure" Elbert and help him find acceptable ways to express strong feelings. This is a fun title for showcasing subject matter from the 100s involving feelings, conduct and magic.

- **Feelings** by Aliki. William Morrow & Co., 1986. 2–4. Aliki puts hand-printed, conversational words in the mouths of expressive, cartoon-style children to explore the world of feelings from a kids' eye view. He covers the gamut of emotions—happiness, humiliation, anger, fear, jealousy, guilt, remorse, loneliness, empathy, grief and boredom. A great introduction to put young students in touch with their feelings.

- **The Feelings Book: The Care & Keeping of Your Emotions** by Dr. Lynda Madison, illustrated by Norm Bendell. Pleasant Company Publications, 2002. 4–6. This book accomplishes similar goals to the previous title, but for older students. Produced by American Girl, the voices and pictured characters are female. But the information about emotions pertains to boys as well. This title also explores a wide range of feelings, with more analysis and guidance for managing emotions.

- **Fishing for Methuselah** by Roger Roth. HarperCollins, 1998. 2–6. Ivan and Olaf are best friends, though you'd never know it from the way they argue and compete. The biggest contest of all is to catch the legendary monster fish, Methuselah. But the competition gets out of hand, and Methuselah himself comes through to save them both. A clever story of friendship, competition and cooperation.

- **Little Women Next Door** by Sheila Solomon Klass. Holiday House, 2000. 3–6. Timid Susan's world is brightened and broadened when Louisa May Alcott's family moves in next door. The Alcotts' attempt to create an ideal community based on the philosophy of transcendentalism, while flawed and short-lived, exposes Susan to experiences of kindness, acceptance and mindful living that help heal the wounds of a difficult childhood.

- *Mr. Emerson's Cook* by Judith Byron Schachner. Penguin Putnam, 1998. 2–6. Ralph Waldo Emerson, poet and philosopher, is so nurtured by his relationship with nature that he neglects to feed his body. When his wife advertises for an "extraordinary cook" to tempt her husband to the table, Annie Burns responds. She loves the Emersons, but it takes unlocking her childhood imagination to stimulate Emerson's appetite. This lovely picture book touches on Emerson's philosophy and explores nature, imagination and friendship. Cameo appearances by Henry David Thoreau and Louisa May Alcott add to the fun and historical depth.

- *The Mystery of Haunted Houses* by Chris Oxlade. Heinemann Library, 1999. 4–6. This volume from the Can Science Solve? series takes a scientific look at the concepts and some specific reports of ghosts and hauntings. The objective tone lends credibility as the author explores both possible explanations and truly mysterious phenomena. The call for a combination of open-mindedness and scientific rigor is healthy and encouraging. An appealing, well-designed series.

- *Night Garden: Poems from the World of Dreams* by Janet S. Wong, illustrated by Julie Paschkis. Simon & Schuster, 2000. 2–6. Gorgeously illustrated, this collection of short poems evokes the elusive, lyrical and sometimes dark world of dreams. There's something compelling about both verse and illustrations that touches the universal experience of dreaming and invites us to open ourselves to its creative magic.

- *Paranormal Powers* by Gary L. Blackwood. Marshall Cavendish, 1998. 4–6. This appealingly designed Secrets of the Unexplained series title introduces extrasensory perception and other unexplained powers of the mind including dowsing, levitation and psychokinesis. The tone is balanced—Blackwood presents examples of paranormal accomplishments, theories put forth to explain them and efforts to validate them that succeeded and failed. In the end, more questions are asked than answered and the effect is satisfyingly mysterious.

- *Picture Puzzler* by Kathleen Westray. Houghton Mifflin, 1994. 2–6. Westray introduces the world of optical illusions created by the ingenious ways our minds work to interpret visual information in this boldly illustrated picture book. Great for use in a lesson or for exploration at a learning center.

- *Stormy Night* by Michele LeMieux. Kids Can Press, 1999. 3–6. This charming sketchbook-style extended picture book shares the night-long musings of a young girl unable to sleep because "too many questions are buzzing through my head." Those questions run the gamut of human feelings and experience with innocence and wit. In the end, though "the big questions" are unanswered and the uneasy feelings remain, the universality of the questions is comforting.

- *A Young Person's Guide to Philosophy* edited by Jeremy Weate, illustrated by Peter Lawman. DK Publishing, 1998. 5–6. Weate begins with a working definition: "A philosopher is somebody who is puzzled by the world, and then asks questions about it." He then describes the boundaries of philosophy: "Philosophy explores what we don't know. When answers are found, philosophy becomes science." This premise aids the discussion to follow, which gives samples of the kinds of questions philosophers ask and then introduces many of history's great philosophers. A good introduction.

Nonprint Resources

- *Mystery of the Senses* produced for PBS Video. WETA Washington, D.C., 1995 (VHS). 5–6. In roughly 10-minute segments, this video introduces both the experiential (psychological) and physical (biological) aspects of each of the five senses. Each segment hinges on a story—the vision segment features a Navajo artist creating a sand painting—that provides context and interest.

Web Resources

- **Dealing With Feelings**
  www.kidshealth.org/kid/feeling/index.html

- **"Here, Madam!!"**
  library.thinkquest.org/3075/noframes.htm
  A visually rich site with concise introductions to the major branches and history of philosophy for older students. If you are unable to access the Web address, visit ThinkQuest (www.thinkquest.org) and search the Internet Challenge Library by site title.

- **Of Mind and Matter: The Mystery of the Human Brain**
  library.thinkquest.org/TQ0312238
  The Psychology section contains good information on psychoanalysis, dreams, emotions, learning, etc., for older students. If you are unable to access the Web address, visit ThinkQuest (www.thinkquest.org) and search the Internet Challenge Library by site title.

- **The Random Acts of Kindness Foundation**
  www.actsofkindness.org
  This is mainly a teacher's site, with activities and lesson plans that support classroom study of kindness as an aspect of character.

Activities for the 100s

Use these activities in the media center or classroom, as parts of a single-period library lesson or in cooperation with classroom teachers. The ideas address standards across the curriculum.

- **Story.** Read aloud *Mr. Emerson's Cook*. Ask the class to identify parts of the story that relate to the Dewey 100s category. Students might notice that Mr. Emerson was a philosopher who asked questions about man and his relationship to nature and the world, or that Annie had to study how Mr. Emerson behaved and how his mind worked (psychology), and use her imagination (also an aspect of psychology) to get him to eat.

- **Dewey 100s Word Scramble.** Have students unscramble words related to the DDC 100s, using the worksheet on page 30.

- **Math Tie-in: Logic Puzzles.** Explain that the study of logic—the mental skill of solving problems in a systematic way—is assigned a Dewey Decimal number of 160. Find a logic riddle to pose to older students, and challenge them to solve it before your next class. You might have several such riddles or puzzles in reserve for interested students to pick up in the media center and return to you with their solutions. **Note:** Lewis Carroll's book *Alice's Adventures in Wonderland* has several such riddles. Suggest that classroom teachers extend this activity into math classes by using logic puzzles that involve mathematical concepts. An excellent source of such puzzles is Part 4 of *Math for Smarty Pants* by Marilyn Burns (Little, Brown and Company, 1982). This book is part of the Brown Paper School series and is widely available.

- **Rhyme.** Copy (enlarge and laminate if you wish) on card stock and cut into 10 horizontal strips the pattern on page 31. Add tape or Velcro to the back of each strip. Then assemble the picture on felt board, one piece per line, as you recite this rhyme about the Dewey 100s:

Who am I, really, and then who are you?

What is for real? Is the sky truly blue?

Spooks, ghosts and witches—where do they fit?

Does my mind have strange powers? What's the truth of it?

What's right and what's wrong? Can I reason it out?

Do my dreams hold the answers to what life's about?

Who were the great thinkers, and what did they see?

Did they sometimes feel silly or sad, just like me?

To explore these great mysteries, to be wise and to know, The Dewey 100s are the place to go!

- **Story: When Seeing Isn't Believing.** Introduce the book *Picture Puzzler* and share some pages that work well with a group. Explain that part of the broad subject of psychology included in the Dewey 100s is the study of how our minds work—specifically how our brains interpret what our senses perceive. Invite students to have fun exploring the book on their own.

- **Visual Arts/Language Arts Tie-in: Your Own Stormy Night.** Introduce and share the beginning of *Stormy Night* and/or *Night Garden: Poems from the World of Dreams*. Then have students create their own two-page spreads expressing "big questions," important feelings or dream experiences in words and visual images. Display the results in the library.

- **Book Reviews.** Work with classroom teachers to offer students an option to earn extra credit by reading fiction books related to Dewey 100s subjects and turning in written book reviews and/or illustrations. Display the results in the media center. Suggest *The Boy Who Could Fly Without a Motor, Little Women Next Door, Fishing for Methuselah, Mr. Emerson's Cook* or other titles of your choosing.

- **Science Tie-in: Experiment in ESP.** Try scientist J. B. Rhine's method of testing students' extrasensory powers using the instructions found on pages 28–29 of *Paranormal Powers*.

- **Math Tie-in: Fractions, Percentages and Probability.** After the Experiment in ESP, suggest that classroom teachers help students calculate their scores as fractions or percentages that express the relationship between correct guesses and total tries. Then compare those fractions or percentages to the scores you would expect based on simple mathematical probability.

- **Visual Arts Tie-in: Expressing Emotions.** Work with classroom or art teachers to share *Feelings.* Then have the class create works of visual art that represent emotions. Students might either draw faces expressing given emotions or create more abstract representations.

- **Story/Creative Challenge.** Read aloud *Elbert's Bad Word.* Then challenge students to come up with their own "strong words" to express strong feelings. Clarify that, like Elbert's new expressions at the end of the book, they must be words that won't offend people or get them in trouble! Have fun sharing students' expressions and encourage them to put the expressions to work as helpers in managing their emotions.

- **Extra Credit Research/History Tie-in.** In cooperation with classroom teachers, invite students to use classroom and media center resources to learn all they can about a famous psychologist, philosopher or philosophical movement from the past or present. Students should prepare written or recorded reports about their subjects, including visual elements like portraits or appropriate symbols, to be displayed in the media center. *A Young Person's Guide to Philosophy* is a good place to start. Students might study *Confucius* as an example of the Dewey 180s; or explore the famous students of transcendentalism in Concord, Massachusetts, at the time of the Civil War, including Ralph Waldo Emerson, Henry David Thoreau and Louisa May Alcott's family, as an example of the 190s. If students go online, enter the Ask Jeeves Kids Web site, and type in "How can I learn about psychologists?" they'll get a list of appropriate names to search. Alternatively, offer students the opportunity to research a famous "haunting" story, like that of Glamis Castle in Scotland or the "Flying Dutchman" ghost ship. A good starting place is *The Usborne Book of Ghosts & Hauntings* by Anna Claybourne (Usborne Publishing, LTD., 1999).

- **Science Tie-in: The Five Senses.** Show one of the five lessons on the *Mystery of the Senses* video. Accompany the lesson with a related sensory experience, like a scent to pass around or a small taste treat. Explain to students that, like many complex subjects, sensory perception can be thought of in at least two different ways—how we experience and interpret sensory input, and the scientific explanation. Show students examples of materials about the senses in both the Dewey 150s and the science section (500s) of your media center or library.

Dewey 100s Word Scramble

Unscramble the following words related to subjects in the Dewey 100s by drawing lines from the scrambled word in the left column to its unscrambled match in the right column.

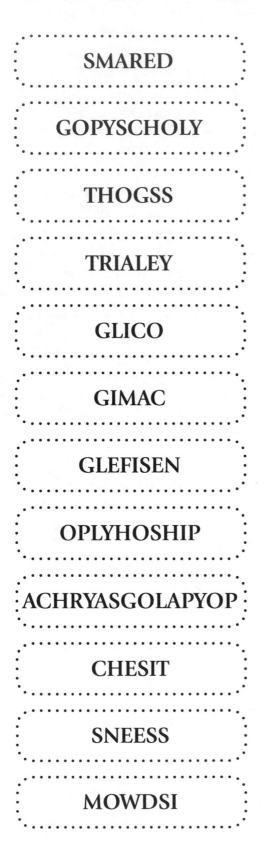

SMARED	DREAMS
GOPYSCHOLY	LOGIC
THOGSS	PHILOSOPHY
TRIALEY	FEELINGS
GLICO	SENSES
GIMAC	GHOSTS
GLEFISEN	PSYCHOLOGY
OPLYHOSHIP	ETHICS
ACHRYASGOLAPYOP	REALITY
CHESIT	PARAPSYCHOLOGY
SNEESS	WISDOM
MOWDSI	MAGIC

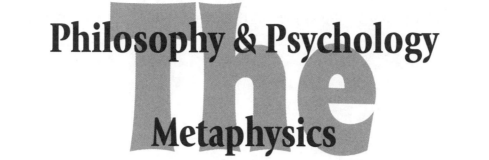

Philosophy & Psychology

Metaphysics

Knowledge, Causation & Humankind

Paranormal Psychology

Philosophical Doctrines

General Psychology

Logic

Ethics

Ancient, Medieval & Eastern Philosophy

Modern Western Philosophy

200s: Religion: Thinking About God

The Dewey 200s look at God and religion. Again, the principal of moving from general to specific is at work because the idea of God is arguably the biggest concept of all. For those who believe in God, faith affects every part of their lives and how they think about everything in the universe.

Along with the most common expressions of religious beliefs in our communities and our country, the Dewey 200s cover ideas about divine mysteries of nature, the many different religions of the world, mythology and ancient stories about creation and the gods. As big a thinker and as dedicated a scholar as he was, Mr. Dewey's limited experience of diverse beliefs shows in his assignment of most of the category to a detailed examination of Christianity, leaving only the 200s, 210s and 290s to consider other belief systems.

Do you have things that are very special to you because they represent your deepest questions and beliefs, the life of your spirit or your family's religious traditions? These might include a Bible, a photograph of your family celebrating a religious holiday, prayer beads or a rock you found in the country on a day when you felt very close to the wonders and mysteries of nature. Putting these things together in a special place is a little like Mr. Dewey giving the 200s category over to an examination of our thoughts about religion and spirituality.

These are the tens groups in the 200s category:

- 200s: General Works about Religion

- 210s: Natural Theology, Theory of Religion (The study of divine qualities in nature.)

- 220s: The Bible

- 230s: Christian Theology

- 240s: Christian Moral and Devotional Teachings

- 250s: Christian Orders & the Local Church (Christian clergy and communities.)

- 260s: Christian Social Teachings

- 270s: Christian History

- 280s: Christian Denominations & Sects

- 290s: Other Religions of the World

Here are some resources to help you explain and explore the Dewey 200s. They, along with other titles from your collection, could be placed on display or built into lesson plans. Religious literature for children often takes the form of stories—parables or moral tales that convey in simple terms aspects of religious history or moral principles. Countless titles tell stories for children from sacred scriptures of Judaism, Buddhism, Christianity and other faiths. You'll find examples in any public library. I've included some that are typical of the genre or that take unusual approaches. In the interests of inclusiveness, and sensitivity about presenting religious content in schools, I have tried to stress multi-faith resources and to provide a wide range of views. Please pick and choose according to local needs.

Print Resources

- **The Book of Goddesses** by Kris Waldherr. Beyond Words Publishing, 1996. 2–6. Women are notably underrepresented in religious literature, for a variety of reasons. This title lends some balance through beautifully illustrated and simply told introductions to 26 legendary goddesses from cultural traditions all over the world. Individual stories could work well for classroom or library lessons; taken together, they might inspire a new sense of power and curiosity in girls, especially.

- **Buddha Stories** by Demi. Henry Holt & Company, 1997. 2–6. The illustrations and book design, as well as the stories themselves, reflect beautiful, time-honored traditions of Buddhist storytelling. These moral tales are brief, powerful, accessible and characteristic of the values of kindness, moderation, wisdom and integrity in Buddhist theology and doctrine.

- **The Children's Illustrated Encyclopedia of Heaven** by Anita Ganeri. Element Children's Books, 1999. 2–6. This well designed book explores concepts of heaven in the broadest context. It offers glimpses of different faiths' teachings about heaven and looks at issues of living and dying; near-death experiences; myths, legends and sacred places associated with heaven; heaven as expressed in the arts; heavenly beings; and parallel ideas about hell. An ambitious reference book that manages to be accessible, appealing and respectful of children and diverse beliefs.

- **Creation: Read-Aloud Stories from Many Lands** retold by Ann Pilling, illustrated by Michael Foreman. Candlewick Press, 1997. 2–6. Luminous illustrations—both dreamy and forceful—complement 16 creation stories from diverse cultural traditions. Individual stories are perfect for classroom or library lessons. A worthy, if less comprehensive and scholarly, competitor to Virginia Hamilton's Newbery Honor book, *In the Beginning*.

- **The Dead Sea Scrolls** by Ilene Cooper. William Morrow & Co., 1997. 5–6. This picture book sized chapter book shares the discovery, recovery and study of the Dead Sea Scrolls and ruins of the Qumran community. While not riveting reading for everyone, those with curiosity about history, archaeology or the scientific analysis of artifacts will find much to enjoy.

- **In Every Tiny Grain of Sand: A Child's Book of Prayers and Praise** collected by Reeve Lindbergh, illustrated by Christine Davenier, Bob Graham, Anita Jeram and Elisa Kleven. Candlewick Press, 2000. 2–6. Simple, moving prayers and quotations from many sources and faith traditions set off by lovely illustrations convey timeless, universal spiritual values of harmony with God, the earth and each other.

- *Islam* by Philip Wilkinson. DK Publishing, 2002. 3–6. Like other titles in the Eyewitness Books series, this book offers readers short "info bites" and a myriad of images in exploring its subject. It covers basic teachings and history of Islam, as well as conquests and cultural achievements of Muslim nations. An appealing introduction to this prominent religion which is often misunderstood in the Western world.

- *Many Waters* by Madeleine L'Engle. Random House, 1998. 4–6. When 15-year-old twins Sandy and Dennys Murry are accidentally transported to early Biblical times they encounter mythical beasts, get involved with Noah's family and struggle to escape before the imminent Great Flood. The final volume of L'Engle's classic Time Quartet, this entertaining, thoughtful fantasy can be read alone—a treat for students as yet unfamiliar with L'Engle's brand of literary magic.

- *Next Year in Jerusalem: 3000 Years of Jewish Stories* retold by Howard Schwartz, illustrated by Neil Waldman. Viking, 1996. 2–6. Waldman's soft lines and muted colors support the gentle messages in this collection of stories designed to share Jewish history and ethical tradition.

- *On Shabbat* by Cathy Goldberg Fishman, illustrated by Melanie W. Hall. Simon & Schuster, 2001. 2–6. Joyful, light-filled illustrations complement a young girl's recounting of the events that make Shabbat "different from every other day" for her family. A beautiful introduction to "the most important Jewish holiday."

- *Parables: Stories Jesus Told* by Mary Hoffman, illustrated by Jackie Morris. Dial, 2000. 3–6. Some of Jesus's stories in the New Testament are hard to understand. Hoffman confronts the challenge of understanding Jesus's moral messages with honesty and quiet wisdom. Text and illustrations are straightforward and eloquent. An effective look at Christ's teachings in practice.

- *Places of Power* by Michael Demunn, illustrated by Noah Buchanan. Dawn Publications, 1997. 2–4. This simple picture book asserts that the earth is full of places where receptive people might experience meaningful spiritual connections with the Creator. While distinctly Native American in tone, the book exudes simple reverence and respect for people of all ages, beliefs and cultures.

- *Send Me Down a Miracle* by Han Nolan. Harcourt, 1996. 5–6. Fourteen-year-old Charity has always been content with her life in small town Alabama. But things are changing. Her mother deserts the family; her artistic and self-discovery instincts are aroused by an exciting, controversial visiting artist; and her adoring relationship with her intense preacher father is strained by claims of miracles which make enemies of preacher and artist, and split the community in two.

- *What I Believe: A Young Person's Guide to the Religions of the World* by Alan Brown and Andrew Langley. Lerner Publishing Group, 1999. 3–6. This friendly guide looks at religion through the eyes of fictional, cartoon-style children. It presents their understanding of the history, teachings and practices of their religious communities in photographs, drawings and simple, clear text. An excellent starting place for research.

- *Women of the Bible: With Paintings from the Great Art Museums of the World* by Carol Armstrong. Simon & Schuster, 1998. 3–6. Two-page spreads of engaging and concise text and related works of art introduce 17 stories of women from the Old Testament, Apocrypha and New Testament. A beautiful book that might inspire students to seek out the original stories.

- ***A World Treasury of Myths, Legends and Folktales: Stories from Six Continents*** retold by Renata Bini, illustrated by Mikhail Fiodorov. H. N. Abrams, 2000. 2–6. Lushly illustrated, this sizable volume shares stories from classical mythology along with offerings from indigenous cultures, Hindu tradition and other less-known sources. The diversity and universality of the stories enhance the book's appeal. Like other stories rooted in exploration of the human spirit, they stress issues of good and evil, and the virtue of seeking harmony with all living things.

Nonprint Resources

- ***Beautiful World*** by Take 6. Warner Brothers Records, Inc., 2002 (music CD). 2–6. The celebrated Christian jazz group shares popular songs from the 1960s–80s with spiritual messages, in styles that include blues, gospel and soul. The choice of material and lush harmonies make for an uplifting, high quality musical experience.

- ***A Fine White Dust*** by Cynthia Rylant, narrated by Jeff Woodman. Recorded Books, Inc., 1997 (audiocassettes). 5–6. Woodman's moving narration of this Newbery Honor Book conveys the yearning and anguish of Pete Cassidy, a 13-year-old boy whose attraction to spirituality makes him vulnerable to the charisma of an irresponsible itinerant revival preacher. Rylant's story treats with equal respect Pete's sincere religious quest, his best friend's avowed atheism and his parents' ambivalence about his experiences.

- ***How Do You Spell God?*** based on the book by Rabbi Marc Gellman and Monsignor Thomas Hartman, written by Barry Harman. HBO Kids Video, 1996 (VHS). 2–6. This provocative, insightful collection of animated stories and children's reflections reveals the diversity and creativity of children's ideas about God, life and death. With frankness and an inclusive spirit, concepts from different faith traditions mingle with doubts about the existence of God. An outstanding and uplifting tribute to the depth of children's thoughts.

Web Resources

- **A Bow of the Head**
  library.thinkquest.org/28505/inde1.html
  An inviting site that offers brief articles on five major world religions, quotes from their scriptures, lists of resources and links to other sites. If you are unable to access the Web address, visit ThinkQuest (www.thinkquest.org) and search the Internet Challenge Library by site title.

- **BrainPOP Religion**
  www.brainpop.com
  Choose "Religion" from the Social Studies category. A fun page offering several activities including a movie, quiz, forum for submitting questions and activity page. This is a subscription site, but it allows visitors some preselected free activities each day and a one-time free trial subscription.

- **Mythology**
  www.windows.ucar.edu/tour/link=/mythology/mythology.html
  A rich and appealing student-created site that explores world mythology through references to heavenly bodies, world maps, family trees of gods and goddesses, etc.

Activities for the 200s

Use these activities in the media center or classroom, as parts of a single-period library lesson or in cooperation with classroom teachers. The ideas address standards across the curriculum.

- **Story.** Choose a story from one of the compilations in the chapter bibliography. Especially appropriate for media center or classroom use are *Buddha Stories, Creation* or *A World Treasury of Myths, Legends and Folktales.* Invite students to summarize for you the moral or spiritual message of the story as they understand it, and discuss how the story fits into the Dewey 200s.

- **Dewey Decimal 200s Crossword Puzzle.** Have students complete the puzzle of words related to religion, using the crossword puzzle on page 40. **Answers:** Across—5. church, 6. revere, 7. mythology, 8. atheist, 9. divine. Down—1. spirit, 2. synagogue, 3. theology, 4. prayer, 7. mosque.

- **Research Opportunity: Religion Survey.** Using the questionnaire on pages 41–42, have students survey their classmates or school communities about religious beliefs and affiliation. Compile and discuss the results.

- **Math Tie-in: Analyzing Survey Results.** Analyzing results of the survey suggested above offers opportunities for students to compile forms and determine numbers and percentages related to measurable aspects of the survey. For example, they might calculate what percent of the children or families surveyed consider themselves Christians, Jews, atheists, undecided, etc.

- **Fingerplay.** Use this fingerplay to introduce the idea of different ways of worshipping whatever we consider sacred. Start by showing each gesture, having ¼ of the class pay special attention to each of gestures 1–4. Tell students that, near the end of the fingerplay, you'll point to each section of the class to repeat its assigned gesture.

  - Some children pray each week in church with gently folded hands. (*Gesture 1: Fold hands together in prayerful gesture.*)

  - Others in a mosque bow down in many different lands. (*Gesture 2: Place forehead on hands crossed flat over each other.*)

  - Across the world, when nighttime comes, folks kneel beside their beds. (*Gesture 3: Place right hand on flat left palm, with thumb, third and fourth fingers folded in and first and second fingers bent at the second knuckle to suggest kneeling knees.*)

  - Still others stand in wood or field with upraised hands and heads. (*Gesture 4: Raise head and hands—palms up—toward ceiling.*)

  - Whatever way we choose to show our love for all that's best. (*Point to each group in turn to repeat its assigned gesture.*)

  - Respect and wonder, search and joy unite us with the rest. (*Gesture 5: Make a circle with hands and arms and end with hands over heart.*)

- **"Q" is for Questions: Creative Thinking.** Introduce this activity by showing part or all of the video *How Do You Spell God?* Then have students write on strips of paper questions they have about God, religion, the origins of life and the world, what happens when we die, different faiths, etc. Do not have students sign their questions. Select questions to display on a bulletin board in the media center, under the heading "The Dewey Decimal 200s: Religion." While you could lead a discussion about where students might look for answers to their questions (and feature media center 200s resources in the process), the goal is not so much to answer the questions as to share ideas about what students are thinking.

- **Discussion/Display: Holy Days and Holidays.** Introduce the concept that every faith has special holidays or holy days using *On Shabbat* or *What I Believe*. Identify holy days or holidays from different faiths that occur during the month of your study of the 200s. Explore in a lesson or display the significance and traditions of each. Invite children of different faiths to share family traditions that celebrate their special days.

- **Book Discussion: Compare and Contrast.** Working with classroom teachers as needed, invite older students to compare *A Fine White Dust* and *Send Me Down a Miracle*. Assign each title to half the students. When they have completed reading or listening to the books, lead a discussion using these prompts:

  - Have one student briefly summarize the plot of *A Fine White Dust*. Then do the same for *Send Me Down a Miracle*.

  - How are the main characters similar and different? How are their situations similar and different?

  - Did you find the experiences, thoughts and feelings of the main character of your story believable? Did they make you understand and care about the character? Why or why not?

  - In each book, an adult comes to town, attracts the main character and creates a crisis in the character's life. Identify these characters in each book, and tell how they affect the protagonists. Have you ever met an adult that affected you so strongly that he or she made you question your beliefs or your ideas about what to do with your life? If so, tell about your experience.

  - How is each story resolved? What do you think are the main things Pete and Charity learn from their experiences?

(Note these passages in the books: *Send Me Down a Miracle*—Chapter 20, page 193, and Chapter 26, pages 235–236; *A Fine White Dust*—Chapter 12 and "Amen," pages 99–100 and 104 in the Aladdin paperback edition.)

- **Composition Learning Center.** This could be done in the media center or classroom. Start by reading selections from *In Every Tiny Grain of Sand*. Then place the book at a learning center and invite students to use it as a model to create their own brief compositions about spiritual or religious issues. Students might compose poems, as on page 13; prayers, as on page 12; or reflections on the beauties of nature, as on page 44 of that title. They could be written or recorded on cassettes, and shared as part of a media center display on the Dewey 200s.

- **Science Tie-in: Analyzing Archaeological Finds.** Suggest to teachers that they review scientific and technological methods used to preserve, restore, date and decipher the Dead Sea Scrolls, described in the book by the same name, as they discuss varied applications of scientific principles and discoveries.

- **Language Arts/Visual Arts Tie-in.** Work with classroom teachers to have students explore the contents of *The Book of Goddesses; Women of the Bible; A World Treasury of Myths, Legends and Folktales;* or other titles in your collection that feature historical or mythical figures related to religion. Have each student choose a figure that interests him or her, write a one-page summary of his or her story and create a work of art portraying that character or some aspect of the story. Display student work in a classroom or the media center.

- **Extra Credit Research Tie-in: The Golden Rule.** In cooperation with classroom teachers, invite students to use classroom and media center resources to learn all they can about the basic ethical law known as the Golden Rule, and how it is expressed in different religious scriptures and traditions. You might either assign each student one religion to research or challenge advanced students to trace the idea through as many faith traditions as possible. The Web site TeachingValues.com **(www.teachingvalues. com.goldenrule.html)** is a good resource. Students might share their findings through charts that show the names and symbols of different religions and the form of the Golden Rule found in each. Charts could be displayed in the classroom or media center.

Dewey 200s
Religion Crossword Puzzle

Across

5. Christian house of worship

6. To show respect for what is sacred

7. Stories of ancient gods and heroes

8. One who does not believe in God

9. Of or relating to God

Down

1. That part of us which is not physical

2. Jewish house of worship

3. Study of God and religion

4. Communication addressed to God

7. Muslim house of worship

Religion Survey

This survey is part of a media center unit studying the Dewey Decimal classification system, specifically the 200s, which cover religion.

Please fill out this survey as completely as possible. You don't need to put your name on it.

1. Do you consider your family to be religious? ☐ YES ☐ NO ☐ SOMEWHAT

2. Do members of your family officially belong to a religious community?

   ☐ YES ☐ NO ☐ SOME MEMBERS DO

3. Which, if any, of the following best describes your family's religious beliefs or affiliations? (Circle all that apply within your family.)

   • Christian

   • Jewish

   • Muslim

   • Buddhist

   • Hindu

   • Baha'í

   • Sikh

   • Atheist

   • Agnostic

   • Other _____

4. On a scale of 1–10, with 10 being the most, how important is religion in the life of your family? _____

5. How often do members of your family participate in organized religious activities?
   ☐ NEVER ☐ OCCASIONALLY ☐ FREQUENTLY

6. What religious holidays or holy days do you observe as a family?

   _____

   _____

7. If your family has a favorite tradition or traditions related to a religious holiday, please share it here: _____

    _____

    _____

8. Do your family members have friends who have different beliefs than those represented in your family? ☐ YES ☐ NO If yes, which category below best describes the beliefs of family friends? (Circle all that apply.)

    • Christian

    • Jewish

    • Muslim

    • Buddhist

    • Hindu

    • Baha'í

    • Sikh

    • Atheist

    • Agnostic

    • Other _____

9. Does your family have a favorite book, music recording, TV show or movie to recommend to other families that carries a religious or spiritual message? If so, please name it here: _____

10. If you wish, use the space below to comment on your family's approach to spiritual or religious issues.

    _____

    _____

    _____

    _____

    _____

Thank you for your cooperation!

300s: Social Sciences: Thinking About Other People

The Dewey 300s cover sociology and anthropology, meaning the study of human society and social relations, from prehistory to the present and speculating into the future. They encompass a huge range of ideas—politics, economics, law, public policy, social movements and institutions, education, commerce, communications, transportation, citizenship, manners, customs and folklore. There are many gray areas. Where is the boundary, for example, between communications and languages (the 400s)? Anthropology and history (the 900s)? Statistics and math (the 510s)? Folklore and mythology (the 290s)? The answer is in applying the subject at hand to examining how people live and work together in groups, but in reality, different libraries might make different choices about the same items.

Ponder this: Your mom needs an office for her new home-based business, so you've just learned that you'll be sharing your room with your little brother. How will you arrange it so you can both find what you need? You'll have to work together and make some rules and compromises that are fair to both of you. Will you keep your things apart, or mix them together? Will his Beanie Babies collection, which he hopes will make him rich someday, be separate from the other stuffed animals in the toy box? How will you choose what music is on the radio? Who will pay for the new things you need to make the room "yours, mine and ours?" As you work out these details, you'll be touching on many of the subject areas Mr. Dewey included in the 300s about people living and working together in groups.

These are the tens groups in the 300s category:

- 300s: General Works about Social Sciences

- 310s: General Statistics

- 320s: Political Science

- 330s: Economics

- 340s: Law

- 350s: Public Administration, Military Science

- 360s: Social Problems and Services, Associations

- 370s: Education

- 380s: Commerce, Communications and Transportation

- 390s: Customs, Etiquette and Folklore

Resources on the 300s

Here are some print and nonprint resources chosen to represent the breadth of the Dewey 300s. They, along with other titles from your collection, could be placed on display or built into your lesson plans.

Print Resources

- ***The Everything Kids' Money Book*** by Diane Mayr. Adams Media Corporation, 2000. 3–6. Everything about this introduction to the history and management of money is fun, from the purple font with green accents to games, jokes and "Fun Facts." There are even math problems and science experiments using coins to sweeten a lively and informative text.

- ***Grandpa's Corner Store*** by DyAnne DiSalvo-Ryan. William Morrow & Co., 2000. 2–3. When a big new supermarket threatens the future of her grandfather's neighborhood grocery, Lucy leads a campaign to save the store. There is much food for thought about realities of commerce and the value of small local businesses in this sweet, simple story.

- ***It's Our World, Too! Young People who are Making a Difference; How they Do it—How You Can, Too!*** by Phillip M. Hoose. Farrar, Straus and Giroux, 2002. 5–6. Part case studies and part handbook, this empowering book shares the passions and achievements of a group of remarkable—but normal—kids who got excited about a cause or project and did something about it. A wonderful look at youthful social activism and organizations that help.

- ***Jobs People Do*** by Christopher Maynard. DK Publishing, 1997. 2–4. This bright, busy picture book shows kids in the roles of chefs, lawyers, plumbers, teachers, etc. Large print and lots of photos make it accessible to young kids in "read-to" or beginning reader modes; middle graders can sample it for solid introductory content. A fun, usable title.

- ***A Life Like Mine: How Children Live Around the World*** written in association with UNICEF. DK Publishing, 2002. 2–6. The different lives of children around the world leap off the pages of this colorful, informative coffee table book. Through real kids' experiences we learn about the current condition of children's rights in the areas of survival, development, protection and participation. The book paints a compelling, and sometimes disturbing, portrait of how children are faring in our global family.

- ***Mary Louise Loses Her Manners*** by Diane Cuneo, illustrated by Jack E. Davis. Random House, 1999. 2–4. This delightfully silly search for Mary Louise's lost manners manages to hint at proper behavior while entertaining kids and adults with a perfect blend of irreverent text and hilarious illustrations.

- ***The Misfits*** by James Howe. Simon & Schuster, 2001. 4–6. Four misfits band together out of a combination of self defense and common interests. While each is uniquely quirky, they are all targets for ridicule in the insecure social world of middle school. When they decide to shake things up by forming a new political party to challenge traditional student council elections, they find the power to effect change in themselves and their world.

- ***Officer Buckle and Gloria*** by Peggy Rathman. Putnam, 1995. 2–4. Caldecott Medal, 1996. Officer Buckle's mission is to share his infinite supply of safety tips with kids. Unfortunately, he's boring and they don't listen—that is, until Gloria, the new police dog, goes along. What will Officer Buckle do when he discovers that his newfound popularity is really about Gloria stealing the show behind his back? Hilarious, delightful and full of safety tips.

- **The Same Sun was in the Sky** by Denise Webb, illustrated by Walter Porter. Northland Publishing, 1995. 2–3. Grandpa explores and interprets petroglyphs in the Arizona desert with his grandson, encouraging him to imagine the Hohokam people who created them. Webb's open-ended approach and Porter's gentle illustrations build empathy and invite us to ponder people's lives in the past and the future. A pleasing, accessible introduction to anthropology appropriate for reading aloud.

- **Silly and Sillier: Read-aloud Tales from Around the World** told by Judy Sierra, illustrated by Valeri Gorbachev. Knopf, 2002. 2–4. Cleverly illustrated and concisely told, these universal tales will get a laugh and make a point. Students will recognize familiar story lines in unfamiliar settings, and delight in the mischief that somehow always manages to come down on the side of the right.

- **The Song of the Molimo** by Jane Cutler. Farrar, Straus and Giroux, 1998. 5–6. Twelve-year-old Harry Jones expects to spend his summer reveling in the wonders of the 1904 St. Louis World's Fair. But his visit takes an unexpected turn when he is involved with an anthropological exhibit—specifically, the unfair treatment of Ota Benga and his fellow African Pygmies. Based on Fair history, the story takes a fascinating look at society's impressive achievements as well as its unenlightened attitudes. Strange and compelling.

- **Turn of the Century** by Ellen Jackson, illustrated by Jan Davey Ellis. Charlesbridge Publishing, 1998. 2–6. This lushly illustrated picture book offers glimpses of life at the turn of each century from 1000 to 2000 AD, in two-page spreads. On the left, a child tells of his or her holiday celebration. On the right is a sampling of habits, gadgets and traditions of the time. Both text and illustrations hint at the increasing rate of change in everything from inventions to attitudes as time goes by. An original idea that invites creative use in the classroom or media center.

- **The U.S. Constitution and You** by Sly Sobel. Barron's Educational Series, Inc., 2001. 2–6. With the look of a reader (small size, large type, lots of illustrations), this thoughtful title introduces the structure of our government as defined in the Constitution, and the reasons behind it all. Concise writing masks sophistication and depth of treatment. An appealing, substantive overview.

- **The View from Saturday** by E. L. Konigsburg. Simon & Schuster, 1996. 4–6. Newbery Medal winner, 1997. Sixth-grade teacher Mrs. Olinski, returning to teaching in a wheelchair after a disabling accident, must choose a class team for the Academic Bowl. Meanwhile, four of her students are forging their own association based on unlikely connections and subtle similarities. This masterpiece of plot, characterization and message explores issues of character, education, cultural acceptance, confidence and learning.

Nonprint Resources

- **The Big Aircraft Carrier** produced by VanDerKloot Films & Television. Little Mammoth Media, 2003 (DVD, VHS). 2–5. Taped footage, accented with cartoon drawings and narrated by a child, explores life and activity aboard a Navy aircraft carrier. This fast-paced, informative video enhances its "kid appeal" by relating statistics to things kids know, like school buses and tall buildings. It touches on the 300s subjects of the military, communications and jobs as well as transportation.

- **Money Rock** by Radford Stone. Disney Presents, 1998 (VHS). 2–6. While this title from the award-winning School House

Rock! series shows its age (it was originally made for TV in 1973) it remains an excellent, fun introduction to basic economics for kids. Eight lively songs explore the history of money, allowance, budgets, bill paying, taxes, investments and the national debt.

Web Resources

- **Aesop's Fables Online Collection**
  www.pacificnet.net/~johnr/aesop/

- **Holidays Around the World for K–12**
  falcon.jmu.edu/~ramseyil/holidays.htm
  This resource site puts you a click away from many pages on the history, traditions and activities connected with holidays of different countries and cultures.

- **Kidsnewsroom.org**
  www.kidsnewsroom.com/newsissues
  This bright, inviting site covers the news with a focus on social issues, politics and government, both nationally and globally.

Activities for the 300s

Use these activities in the media center or classroom, as parts of a single-period library lesson or in cooperation with classroom teachers. The ideas address standards across the curriculum.

- **Story.** Read aloud *Officer Buckle and Gloria.* Ask the class to identify parts of the story that relate to the Dewey 300s. Students might mention that Officer Buckle is a policeman, which is a social service and part of public administration, or that his job involves educating people about safety. You could take the same approach with *Grandpa's Corner Store,* which involves elements of economics and commerce, social activism and education.

- **Dewey 300s Letter Ladder.** Enjoy this vocabulary game using the worksheet on page 51.

- **Games and Tricks: Fun with Money.** Introduce and share bits of trivia from *The Everything Kids' Money Book.* Then demonstrate some of the tricks in the book (e.g., those found on pages 89–90) and pose math challenges like the "Figure this Out" features. Use appropriate problems from the book or make up similar problems at grade level.

- **Song: "How Do People Live Together?"** Sing this song to the tune of "Did You Ever See a Lassie?" Make up your own phrases or invite students to think up additional phrases to add or substitute, keeping in mind the subjects covered in the 300s category.

  How do people live together,
  Together, together,
  How do people live together ,
  All over the world?

  Sample phrases:
  By learning together,
  By choosing our leaders,

  Repeated refrain:
  That's how we live together,
  All over the world.

  Additional phrases:
  By protecting each other,
  By sharing our interests, *(That's how we live together all over the world.)*

  By following rules,
  And minding our manners, *(That's how we live together all over the world.)*

  By working together,
  By buying and selling, *(That's how we live together all over the world.)*

  By helping each other,
  By trading our stories…

  Finish with refrain:
  That's how we live together,
  All over the world.

- **Story: Fairy Tales and Folklore.** Choose a favorite read-aloud story from a book of fairy tales or folktales. You'll find great choices, guaranteed to garner a giggle, in *Silly and Sillier.*

- **Language Arts/Visual Arts Tie-in: Life in 2100.** Review with students *Turn of the Century.* Then place it at a learning center with paper and art supplies and invite students to create their own two-page spread envisioning life in the year 2100. Display their work in the media center.

- **Visual Arts/Language Arts Tie-in: Create a Puppet Play.** Invite interested students to form groups and adapt stories from *Silly and Sillier* into puppet plays. Students can color pictures of their characters on white paper plates and mount them on large craft sticks to make puppets. Paper, tag board or other simple craft materials can be fashioned into sets and props. A draped table can serve as a puppet stage. Have a narrator read the parts of the story not spoken by specific characters. Encourage students to plan appropriate sound effects and use voices that express their characters well. Then sit back and enjoy the show!

- **Book Discussion.** Work with classroom teachers to involve older students in discussing *The Misfits* and *The View from Saturday*. Assign each title to half the class. After reading, divide the class into discussion groups of four to six students, each group evenly split between the two titles. Ask one member of each group to briefly introduce the story and the main characters in *The Misfits*. Do the same for *The View from Saturday*. Than have the groups consider these questions. After discussion, reconvene the class and have each group summarize their thoughts about one of the questions until all have been addressed.

  - What brought each group of students together?

  - How are the two groups similar? How are they different?

  - How do relationships among the main characters change during the stories?

  - What does each group accomplish for its members?

  - How does each group affect other people in the school community?

  - Do these characters remind you of students or groups in your school? In what ways?

  - Which of your book's characters is your favorite? Why?

  - If Julian invited the Gang of Five to join the Souls for tea, what do you think they'd talk about? How would they get along?

- **Science Tie-in: Explaining the Natural World.** Work with classroom teachers to explore the different approaches to explaining the world of nature represented by science and folklore. Explain that people

have always been awed by nature, and have always sought both objective and imaginative ways of understanding and using the natural world. Many folktales reflect attempts to explain or harness natural forces—the animal world, water, fire or, perhaps most often, the sky. Then use opportunities in your curriculum to pair lessons in biology, astronomy, etc., with related folktales. A good place to go for ideas is *Tales of the Shimmering Sky: Ten Global Folktales with Activities* by Susan Milord (Williamson Publishing, 1996), which follows well-told tales with creative, science-based classroom activities.

- **Math Tie-in: Create a Budget.** Math class can offer a perfect tie-in while you examine economics and commerce. Work with teachers to have students create budgets for personal money management—either practical budgets that reflect their real-life income from allowance or odd jobs, or "what-if" budgets that explore how they'll manage their future fortunes! For guidance on creating a budget, look in the 332s in your media center or public library. Two titles that offer help are *Cha-Ching! A Girl's Guide to Spending and Saving* by Laura Weeldreyer (Rosen Central, 1999) and *Money: Earning it, Saving it, Spending it, Growing it, Sharing it* by Steve Otfinoski (Scholastic, 1996).

- **Research Challenge: Where are they Now?** Introduce *It's Our World, Too!* Then invite students to use classroom, media center or Internet resources to update the class on one or more of the social activists or projects featured in the book. The Where Are They Now? worksheet on page 52 can guide their research and shape their reports.

- **Exploring Statistics.** Look up the word "statistics" in a dictionary. You'll find something like this: "A branch of mathematics dealing with collecting, analyzing, interpreting and communicating information expressed as numbers." Why do students think this subject is included in the Dewey 300s? There is no right answer. Perhaps Mr. Dewey wanted to emphasize the objective, systematic study of the social sciences, which often involves using statistics to quantify information for analysis and comparison. Then introduce *A Life like Mine: How Children Live Around the World* and show an example of statistics from the book. Divide the class into four groups. Each will examine one chapter of the book, looking for examples of statistics. Have them make notes about all the statistics they find, including different ways of presenting the number concepts (e.g., through pictures of toy soldiers on pages 84–85). Note that the fourth chapter, "Participation," uses fewer statistics and embeds them more in the text, so you might assign that chapter to a group of diligent, task-oriented students. You will either need to provide a copy of the book for each group, or arrange time so that one group works on this task while the rest do other work. When all groups are finished, reconvene the class and discuss, using these prompts:

- Have each group share one example of statistics in its chapter.

- Why do you think the authors chose to share this information in numerical form? *(Students might mention that statistics can be a fast way of conveying information. They can draw attention to the size of a problem or achievement through big numbers, or make disturbing realities easier to accept by distancing us from human emotions. Encourage a range of ideas.)*

- Which statistics in your chapter surprised or interested you the most? Why?

- What did you learn from studying the statistics in your chapter?

- Which way of presenting the number concepts did you like best? Why?

- **Guest Speaker: Discovering Anthropology.** Invite an anthropologist to introduce the discipline with a focus on his or her specialty and current projects. Prepare the class by reading *The Same Sun was in the Sky* or assigning *The Song of the Molimo* and developing thoughtful questions for their guest. You might ask about anthropological findings related to your area, or changing attitudes about the intelligence and achievements of early humans. Be sure to ask about the use of scientific methods and technology in the practice of anthropology.

Social Sciences Letter Ladder

Use each letter of the alphabet to complete the words and build the letter ladder below. Use each letter only once. All words relate to subjects covered in the Dewey Decimal system 300s.

A B C D E F G H I J K L M N O P Q R S T U V W X Y Z

```
                    __  O T I N G
          F O L  __  L O R E
                E  __  P E N S E S
                A  __  T H R O P O L O G Y
      S T A T I  __  T I C S
          E D U C  __  T I O N
  A S S O C I A  __  I O N
      T R A N S  __  O R T A T I O N
              V O  __  U N T E E R S
  C O M M U N I  __  A T I O N S
              E C  __  N O M I C S
          E T I  __  U E T T E
      C O N S T  __  T U T I O N
      M O N E  __
          C I T I  __  E N S H I P
      G O V E  __  N M E N T
              L A  __
                  __  U S I N E S S
                C  __  S T O M S
          B U D  __  E T
          R I G  __  T S
                  __  A I R Y   T A L E S
          I N V  __  S T M E N T
  P U B L I C   A  __  M I N I S T R A T I O N
                E  __  P L O Y M E N T
                  __  O B S
```

© 2005 by Diane Findlay (UpstartBooks)

Where Are They Now?

Use classroom, media center or Internet resources to update the class on one or more of the social activists or projects featured in *It's Our World, Too! Young People who are Making a Difference.* This worksheet will help guide your research and shape your report.

I chose this social activist: _____

He or she worked on this project: _____

Why I chose this person: _____

_____

What has happened to this person since the book was written? _____

_____

_____

What has happened to his or her project? _____

_____

_____

What other young people or organizations are working on this issue? _____

_____

What was my best source of information on the current status of this person or project?

_____

_____

How could I get involved in carrying on this person's work? _____

_____

_____

_____

_____

400s: Language: Communicating with Words

The study of languages makes up the Dewey 400s. After the range and complexity of concepts in the 300s, this category offers welcome relief. Its scope is limited and clear. It includes study of the origins and history of languages in general, the evolution and structure of individual languages, the process of learning languages and local libraries' collections of works in foreign or multiple languages which might be used in the study of languages.

Again, differences in attitudes from the late 1800s to today and Mr. Dewey's limited experience of the world's countries and cultures show in his assignment of this category's tens groupings. The system is very ethnocentric in its detailed exploration of languages associated with Western civilization and its relegation of all things Eastern to the catch-all 490s. Since all of the top three, and five of the top ten languages with the most native speakers fall into this "other" category (Encarta Online Encyclopedia 2003), Dewey's understandable but outdated vision causes problems for scholars using the system today. Looking at the world's languages

and the difficulties that Dewey's decisions create will seem natural in schools with lots of ethnic diversity. For students in less diverse cultural environments, it can provide a welcome window into the wider world.

In contrast, the 400s showcase an example of Dewey's creative and efficient thinking. Understanding the 400s will give students an advantage when they get to the 800s, where this pattern of classification by geographic/linguistic areas recurs. For example, the 450s look at Italian languages; the 850s examine Italian literature.

It's time for your little brother to move into your room. How will you communicate with each other about how to share the space? Will you draw a line down the center of the room and post signs saying "My Side" and "Your Side"? Will you do the same in the closet? On the dresser? Will you talk in a secret language you share, so your Mom won't know where you keep the stuff you're not supposed to have in your room at all, like that stash of candy at the bottom of the toy box? Maybe you need a more detailed way to organize your things, now that you have twice as much collected in the same space. You could agree to each put your school clothes on the left side of the closet and your sports clothes on the right, and then do the same with your school supplies and sports equipment—school stuff on the left side of the shelves and sports stuff on the right. Okay, no kid cares about being **that** organized! But it's the kind of pattern you'll see in the Dewey 400s. The subjects have to do with how we communicate with each other, and the order in which the numbers are assigned (like your decision to put school stuff on the left and sports stuff on the right) forms a pattern that repeats later in another part of the system.

These are the tens groups in the 400s category:

- 400s: General Works about Language

- 410s: Linguistics (The study of human speech and language.)

- 420s: English

- 430s: Germanic Languages

- 440s: French

- 450s: Italian

- 460s: Spanish & Portuguese

- 470s: Latin

- 480s: Greek

- 490s: Other Languages

Resources on the 400s

Here are some resources to help you discover the Dewey 400s. They, along with other titles from your collection, could be placed on display or built into lesson plans.

Print Resources

- ***A is for Aarrgh!*** by William J. Brooke. HarperCollins, 1999. 4–6. This hilarious novel looks at the Stone Age beginnings of spoken and written language and tells a good story about human ingenuity, treachery and the ultimate triumph of good. Students will giggle as they watch familiar personality types emerge and share in the upheaval caused by Mog's revolutionary practice of creating mouth sounds to name things.

- ***Alphabetical Order: How the Alphabet Began*** by Tiphaine Samoyault. Viking, 1998. 4–6. Beautifully designed and illustrated, this slim, inviting history of the world's alphabets and writing systems almost reads like fiction. Lively and engaging text delivers an impressive overview of the subject without sounding didactic. The lush, elegant visuals may send students running for calligraphy pens, and the inclusion of nonverbal languages (American Sign Language, Morse code, Braille and Semaphores) widens its appeal.

- ***Faith and the Electric Dogs*** by Patrick Jennings. Scholastic, 1996. 3–5. This imaginative story combines character drama and science fiction, with an appealing language twist. Faith's family has moved to Mexico, which she hates for its strangeness of language and culture. She teams up with Edison the "electric dog"—Spanish idiom for mutt—in an attempt to return to California by rocket, with surprising results. Language permeates the book's design as well as content, in the form of margin notes that translate bits of Spanish and "Bowwow" (dog language) from the text.

- ***Home at Last*** by Susan Middleton Elya, illustrated by Felipe Davalos. Lee & Low Books, 2002. 2–6. Ana's family are Mexican immigrants to the U.S. They experience difficult adjustments to their new home in this warm, honest, optimistic picture book. The focus is on Mama's challenges dealing with the language barrier and small triumphs as she struggles to learn English, which eventually make her adopted country feel like home. A good awareness and empathy builder.

- ***In English, of Course*** by Josephine Nobisso, illustrated by Dasha Ziborova. Gingerbread House, 2002. 2–6. Josephine, an Italian immigrant, tries to tell her ESL class about her life in Italy, in English. What results, with the help of an encouraging teacher, is a hilarious story of her misadventures on a farm. The busy, playful illustrations and story-within-a-story format provide delightful insights into the joys and challenges of learning a second language.

- ***The Language of Birds*** by Rafe Martin, illustrated by Susan Gaber. Putnam, 2000. 2–6. In this Russian tale, young Ivan rescues a baby bird and is granted, as a reward, knowledge of the language of birds. Access to their wisdom aids Ivan and his family in unexpected ways. A lushly illustrated, satisfying story.

- ***Lu & Clancy's Secret Languages*** by Louise Dickson, illustrated by Pat Cupples. Kids Can Press, 2001. 1–4. In this Lu & Clancy series title, the canine detectives are on the trail of Leonardo and Grump, burglars who specialize in secret languages. The simple plot provides a framework for introducing fun ways for kids to share secrets—from hand signs and gestures through invisible writing and a series of spoken codes. Younger students will enjoy trying these languages and making up their own.

- ***More Simple Signs*** by Cindy Wheeler. Viking, 1998. 2–6. This book (and its predecessor, *Simple Signs*) presents American Sign Language standard signs for 30 everyday words and phrases, giving context, written hints about use and clear illustrations. It's an inviting introduction that may encourage students to seek out other signs and build sentences on their own.

- ***Punctuation Power: Punctuation and How to Use it*** by Marvin Terban. Scholastic, 2000. 3–6. In its slim paperback version, this is about as appealing as student handbooks get. The friendly font, helpful use of color, amusing drawings and light tone all support a well-designed format with lots of solid information that's easy to access. A winner!

- ***Seeker of Knowledge: The Man Who Deciphered Egyptian Hieroglyphics*** by James Rumford. Houghton Mifflin, 2000. 2–6. Dreamy watercolors and sharp hieroglyphic images set the tone of this picture book telling the story of Jean-Francois Champollion, who unlocked the secrets of ancient Egypt for the world's scholars by decoding the languages on the Rosetta Stone.

- ***Sequoyah's Gift: A Portrait of the Cherokee Leader*** by Janet Klausner. HarperCollins, 1993. 4–6. With respect, evenness of tone and honesty about the confusion of fact with legend, Klausner portrays the life and accomplishments of the only human ever known to create a written language system without first being literate in some language! A fascinating story, sensitively told.

- ***There's a Frog in my Throat: 440 Animal Sayings a Little Bird Told Me*** by Loreen Leedy and Pat Street. Holiday House, 2003. 2–6. A clever riot of a picture book, this collection of common English sayings using animal references entertains from the jacket text to "the tail end." There's no end to the creative responses it might inspire!

- ***Under, Over, by the Clover: What is a Preposition?*** by Brian P. Cleary, illustrated by Brian Gable. Lerner Publishing Group, 2002. 2–3. It's hard to find a more fun way to introduce the mechanics of the English language than Cleary's Words are CATegorical series. In this title, delightfully silly animal characters act out the rhyming text, which is printed in a large, wacky font that emphasizes prepositions in bright colors. A great read-aloud title.

- ***Who Ordered the Jumbo Shrimp? And Other Oxymorons*** by Jon Agee. Farrar, Straus and Giroux, 2002. 2–6. While "oxymoron" is a very big word for a second grader, the concept is clearly and amusingly demonstrated in this simple little book. Agee's black-and-white cartoon-style illustrations illuminate the contradictions in such expressions as "resident alien" (a spaceman washing his spaceship on the street outside his suburban home) and "light heavyweight" (a bulky boxer held aloft by the breeze from a rotating fan). Great fun in itself, this book might motivate students to explore other odd forms of expression in our language.

Nonprint Resources

- ***Grammar Rock*** by David B. McCall. Disney Presents, 1997 (VHS). 2–6. Like the School House Rock! title used in the previous chapter, this fun educational video was made in the 1970s for TV and recently released on VHS for a new generation. It holds up admirably doing what this series does so well—introducing concepts through clever, catchy songs. Here, the songs explain the roles of several parts of speech.

- ***Pick Me Up! Fun Songs for Learning Signs*** by Sign2Me. Northlight Communications, Inc., 2003. 2–3. This multimedia kit (book plus music and video CDs) offers detailed instructions for sharing ASL signs along with 20 original songs. While some of the songs are geared to babies and toddlers, many are appropriate for younger elementary students. A wonderful resource that, with a little preparation, could add a fun twist to library lessons.

- ***The Story of Doctor Doolittle*** by Hugh Lofting, narrated by Nadia May. Blackstone Audiobooks, 2000 (audiocassette). 4–6. This classic tale, which puts the recent movies to shame for creativity and charm, tells of the kindly doctor whose love for animals and gift for speaking their languages leads him into all kinds of trouble and fascinating adventures. It's worth reclaiming and sharing in its original form with today's students; May's narration is irresistible.

- **Merriam-Webster for Kids Word Central**
  www.wordcentral.com/home.html
  This appealing interactive site offers a daily "buzzword," dictionary, thesaurus, word games and more.

- **Online Hieroglyphics Translator**
  www.quizland.com/hiero.htm
  Students will enjoy seeing words and phrases translated to Egyptian hieroglyphics, and reading the explanations of the pictographs used.

- **Say Hello to the World**
  www.ipl.org/div/kidspace/hello
  This eye-opening site gives kids access to a simple greeting in many languages, including sign language and Braille. A fun way to introduce the multiplicity of world languages.

Activities for the 400s

Use these activities in the media center or classroom, as parts of a single-period library lesson or in cooperation with classroom teachers. The ideas address standards across the curriculum.

Note: You might create a display to visually demonstrate the problems caused by Dewey's choices of subject matter for the tens groupings within Languages. Divide the bulletin board into ten same-sized sections. Label them 400, 410, 420, etc. Then place in each a word or symbol that expresses the content of that grouping. You might use a picture of a dictionary for 400 and one of the Rosetta Stone for 410. Then write a simple greeting ("Hello") in English under 420. Do the same for the remaining groupings, in the appropriate languages. When you get to the 490s, include the greeting in 5–10 languages which fall into this category. The Say Hello to the World Web site on page 57 will provide the greetings. You could use the display to stimulate discussion about how Mr. Dewey saw the world in the late 1800s, compared to how we see it now.

- **Story.** Read aloud a grade-appropriate story from the chapter bibliography. *Home at Last; In English, of Course* or *The Language of Birds* are good choices. Then talk about the importance of language in our everyday lives.

- **Mystery Morse Code Message.** Decipher a coded message. Use the Mystery Morse Code game sheet on page 60. To increase the challenge for older students, consider giving the message using audible tones or visible light signals. The message is: "We all smile in the same language."

- **Sing and Sign.** Demonstrate and teach children to sign along to a simple children's song. *Pick Me Up! Fun Songs for Learning Signs* will get you started. Then invite children to figure out how to sign the main ideas in other simple songs they know, using a standard sign language dictionary, to share at the next lesson. "Row, Row, Row Your Boat" is an easy one to figure out together.

- **Research Opportunity: Language Survey.** Using the Languages Survey on pages 61–62, have students survey their classmates or school communities about the languages spoken in their homes or families. Compile and discuss the results.

- **Visual Arts Tie-in: Illustrating Expressions.** Introduce both *There's a Frog in my Throat* and *Who Ordered the Jumbo Shrimp?* Then have students select an expression or figure of speech and use these books as models to create a clever work of visual art that illustrates it.

- **Discussion: Origins and Use of Language.** Have students read *A is for Aarrgh!* and *Alphabetical Order,* or assign half the class to read each book. Then lead a discussion about the origins of language using these prompts:

  - How did people communicate before spoken language?

  - How did people remember things or share complex messages before written language?

  - Name some advantages Mog and his tribe find as they begin to use spoken language. Name some disadvantages.

  - What are the advantages of using written language? What disadvantages can you think of?

  - Based on your reading and your own experience, suggest positive or constructive ways that spoken and written language are used today. Then suggest negative or damaging ways language is used.

- How does literacy (the ability to read and write) help an individual? A community? The world?

- What would happen if everyone learned to speak and write two languages—their native tongue and a second, global language taught and used all over the world? How would sharing a world language change things?

- **Game: Crack the Code.** Divide the class into teams and assign each team one of the secret written languages in *Lu & Clancy's Secret Languages.* Give each team a different simple sentence to translate into their assigned language. Then collect and redistribute their work, making sure that no team gets its own message. Use a stopwatch or timer to see how long it takes the teams to translate the messages back to English. To increase the challenge, play a second round in which teams create and use their own secret languages to code their messages. If their languages are not fairly transparent, like most of the languages in the book, they should either provide a key to their codes with their translated sentences, or present and explain their work to the class.

- **Booktalks.** Assign students to read (or listen to) *The Story of Doctor Doolittle, A is for Aarrgh!, Faith and the Electric Dogs* or *Sequoyah's Gift.* Students will prepare brief (one to two minute) talks for the class, designed to entice others to read their book. Booktalks are similar to oral book reports, but less analytical and more entertaining. They often end with a cliff-hanger. For a fun follow-up activity, poll the class to see who plans to read which book, based on which booktalk.

- **Composition Learning Center.** Either read aloud from the book, or cue up and play from the audiocassette excerpts from *The Story of Doctor Doolittle* which involves conversation between the Doctor and animals. Then leave the tape and the book at a learning center for students to explore. Challenge students to imagine themselves with the gift of speaking to animals. What animal would they like to talk to? What would they say? Have them create conversations between themselves and animals as skits to share with the class.

- **Math Tie-in.** Encourage teachers to discuss the specialized and global language of mathematics during math lessons, pointing out its use of letters from the Greek alphabet and other symbols not used in standard English.

- **Science Tie-in.** Invite interested students to research ways that scientific method and technology are used to break codes or learn about the past by deciphering ancient languages. A good place to start is with *Seeker of Knowledge: The Man Who Deciphered Egyptian Hieroglyphics.*

- **Language Arts/Visual Arts Tie-in.** Work with classroom teachers to have students create their own word/letter shape compositions like those at the end of *Alphabetical Order,* or challenge students to develop their own alphabet font that incorporates pictures into the letter shapes.

- **Extra Credit Research/Geography Tie-in: Who Speaks What?** In cooperation with classroom teachers, invite students to use classroom and media center resources to learn all they can about the languages of the world—where and by whom they are spoken. Reports should take the form of maps or charts showing the distribution of languages and numbers of speakers. Start in any general encyclopedia, under Languages.

Mystery Morse Code Message

Use the written symbols for letters in International Morse Code to decipher the hidden message below.

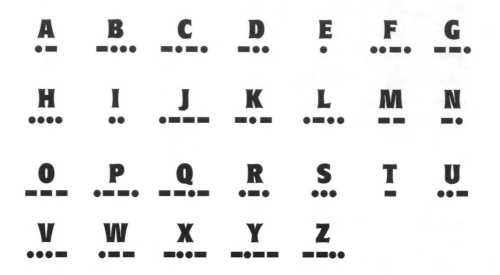

The coded message:

        © 2005 by Diane Findlay (UpstartBooks)

Languages Survey

This survey is part of a media center unit studying the Dewey Decimal classification system, specifically the 400s, which cover languages. Please fill out this survey as completely as possible. You don't need to put your name on it.

1. Does anyone in your family speak a language other than English?

    ☐ YES ☐ NO ☐ JUST LEARNING

2. If so, how many members of your family speak or are studying additional languages? _____

3. What languages other than English do they speak? _____

    _____

    _____

4. What is the main language spoken in your home? _____

    _____

5. If your family includes recent immigrants who speak a language other than English, how important is it to you that children in the family learn the language of the original homeland? (Circle the appropriate number, with 1 meaning unimportant and 5 meaning very important.)

    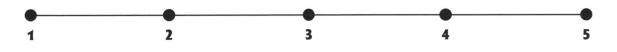

    1   **2**   **3**   **4**   **5**

6. What languages other than English are members of your family studying?

    _____

    _____

7. Why are members of your family studying additional languages? (Check all that apply, write comments if "Other.")

   • To communicate better with friends or relatives from other cultures

   • To fulfill a school requirement

   • To use in their professional lives

   • To use in leisure travel

   • Just for fun

   • Other _____

8. Do you live in a neighborhood in which languages other than English are spoken? ☐ YES ☐ NO If yes, what languages are represented?

   _____

   _____

9. If you wish, use the space below to comment on your feelings about the importance of learning foreign languages.

   _____

   _____

   _____

   _____

   _____

   _____

   _____

   _____

   _____

Thank you for your cooperation!

  © 2005 by Diane Findlay (UpstartBooks)

500s: Science & Mathematics: Studying the Natural World

In the 500s, Dewey tackles mathematics and the natural sciences. *Merriam Webster's Collegiate Dictionary, Tenth Edition* defines mathematics as "the science of numbers and their operations, interrelations, combinations, generalizations and abstractions, and of space configurations and their structure, measurement, transformations and generalizations." That's a mouthful! The same dictionary's definition of science is more concise—it refers to "the state of knowing, as distinguished from ignorance and misunderstanding," and stresses systematic study requiring objectivity and proof. Intuitively, the two go together to represent disciplined, rational, orderly approaches to understanding our world. And while "science" includes astronomy, chemistry, biology, etc., it also implies the process of systematic, disciplined study that can be applied to any subject. Taking an example from the previous chapter, linguistics (410s) is defined as the systematic study of speech and language. In considering the natural sciences, Dewey invites us to study everything in our natural world from the smallest subatomic particles to the expanses of space, and from remote prehistory to theories about the future. Mathematics offers both its own theoretical approach to studying our world, and tools for measuring and quantifying as we conduct those studies.

You and your little brother are having problems sharing your room. He complains that your rock collection and weather lab equipment take up too much space. But, after all, you are older and the room was yours first. Aren't you entitled to more space? And what about his "dinosaur egg" and his "comet rock"? He's convinced the smelly old egg he found in the quarry is that last remaining link with living dinosaurs, and that his gnarled, sparkly rock came from a comet and has magic powers. You know it's nonsense, but try convincing him to get rid of the worthless junk! What's the answer? Should you calculate the area of the room and then assign the space in proportion to your relative ages? Hire a paleontologist to convince him that his rotten egg is just that? Research types of rocks to correctly identify his priceless "comet," or just let him enjoy his own personal science fiction? Each of these solutions involves ideas you can explore in the Dewey 500s—Science and Mathematics.

These are the tens groups in the 500s category:

- 500s: General Works about Science and Mathematics

- 510s: Mathematics

- 520s: Astronomy

- 530s: Physics

- 540s: Chemistry

- 550s: Earth Sciences

- 560s: Paleontology

- 570s: Life Sciences

- 580s: Botany

- 590s: Zoology

Resources on the 500s

Here are some print and nonprint resources related to the 500s. They, along with other titles from your collection, could be placed on display or built into your lesson plans. Rather than mirroring local collections, which are likely to be strong in the popular areas of astronomy, dinosaurs and wild animals, I've chosen to emphasize less familiar sections of the 500s along with unusual but useful approaches to those perennial favorites.

Print Resources

- ***Backpack Books: 1001 Facts about Dinosaurs*** by Neil Clark and William Lindsay. DK Publishing, 2002. 3–6. Dinosaur enthusiasts will revel in the dramatic, realistic illustrations and depth of detail in this little Backpack Books series paperback. Along with ample information about how many different types of dinosaurs evolved, lived and became extinct are lots of quick facts and fun trivia.

- ***Beakman's Book of Dead Guys and Gals of Science*** by Luann Colombo. Andrews McMeel, 1994. 3–6. This colorful, quirky magazine-style book introduces 15 prominent scientists and their work. The biographies are sketchy, but the overall mix of information and humor, photos and drawings is enticing.

- ***The Ben Franklin Book of Easy & Incredible Experiments*** produced by the Franklin Institute Science Museum. John Wiley & Sons, 1995. 3–6. Hundreds of books of science experiments are available for kids. While this one is not flashy, it's appealing for its straightforward explanations, simple directions and use of common household materials. It gives background about Ben Franklin and covers subjects of interest to him including weather, music and sound, paper and printing and scientific inquiry in general.

- ***The Case of the Barfy Birthday*** by Michele Torrey, illustrated by Barbara Johansen Newman. Penguin Putnam, 2003. 2–3. Like Encyclopedia Brown, Doyle and Fossey are the premiere detectives in their fifth grade class. But this dynamic duo uses scientific method and lab analysis to save the day. In this title from their series of early chapter books, find out why Zoe will **not** go to prison for poisoning her sister, why Sloane will **never** be readmitted to the Snob Club and much more! End matter includes discussion of scientific method and activities related to the cases.

- ***Dino Riddles*** by Katy Hall and Lisa Eisenberg, illustrated by Nicole Rubel. Dial, 2002. 2–3. Haven't you always wondered what you'd get if you crossed a dinosaur with a rabbit? (A Tricerahops!) This easy reader is packed with silly riddles and delightful pictures that are perfect for lightening the mood while you spotlight the ever-popular dinosaur section of your 500s collection.

- ***Eco-Fun: Great Projects, Experiments, and Games for a Greener Earth*** by David Suzuki and Kathy Vanderlinden. Douglas & McIntyre, 2001. 3–5. The authors offer 48 activities designed to help children learn about the environment. Chapters dealing with air, water, Earth, the sun's power and plants and animals organize the activities, which are mostly science experiments punctuated with games and offbeat options like "Animal Yoga." Drawings illustrate easy-to-follow directions and the chatty, enthusiastic tone should engage even resistant students.

- ***Math Curse*** by Jon Scieszka and Lane Smith. Viking, 1995. 2–6. A WOW of a picture book! When his math teacher says that almost anything can be thought of as a math problem, one student becomes obsessed—cursed—with viewing everything in his life in mathematical terms. The illustrations are bold and chaotic, reinforcing his growing anxiety; the text is clever and riotous all the way to its hilarious, creative solution. You'll enjoy it along with your students.

- *No Fair!* by Caren Holtzman. Scholastic, 1997. 2–3. This Hello Math Reader series title looks at mathematical probability in the context of two young friends trying to decide what and where to play and how to share. Interesting activities at the end illustrate and apply the math concept.

- *The Number Devil: A Mathematical Adventure* by Hans Magnus Enzensberger, illustrated by Rotraut Susanne Berner. Henry Holt & Company, 1998. 5–6. Strange and intriguing, this book follows the nightly dreams of a young student whose frustration with his math teacher causes him to conjure up a Number Devil. The stereotypical horned rascal is full of tricks of a theoretical math sort, and the book is full of graphic representations and fascinating information about numbers, number series and the mysteries of math. Older students with even a tiny bit of interest in math should latch onto this with enthusiasm.

- *Pass the Energy, Please!* by Barbara Shaw McKinney. Dawn Publications, 2000. 2–6. From the meadow, the ocean, the plains, the woodlands and the Arctic tundra, McKinney introduces the concept of "passing the energy" through food chains. The thoughtful poem inspires wonder as well as respect for nature's cycles of energy transfer.

- *The Salamander Room* by Anne Mazer. Knopf, 1997. 2–4. In this dreamy, richly illustrated picture book, Brian finds a salamander in the woods and brings it home. His mother helps him imagine how he will provide for its needs, until he has created a fantasy habitat in his bedroom. Front notes invite students to become "habitat detectives," carefully observing the complex elements that make up a habitat.

- *The Science Book for Girls and Other Intelligent Beings* by Valerie Wyatt, illustrated by Pat Cupples. Kids Can Press, 1994. 3–6. The upbeat format and fun premise—a wacky, modern-day fairy godmother helps an ordinary girl discover the fascinating science that surrounds her during a typical day—are too good to miss! Bright, silly illustrations mix with routine events, experiments, recipes, games and challenges to lure kids into discovering and enjoying the science of everyday life. Sidebars profile a collection of women scientists.

- *Starry Messenger: Galileo Galilei* by Peter Sís. Farrar, Straus and Giroux, 1996. 2–6. Gloriously designed, this Caldecott Honor book tells of a baby born in Italy in 1564 "with stars in his eyes." His name was Galileo. He challenged the beliefs of the day to assert that the earth moved around the sun, and not the other way around. He was condemned by the church and lived his life under house arrest for believing and teaching what he could see with his own eyes. But he was true to his convictions and was, eventually, vindicated. A rich experience that could stimulate meaningful discussion.

- *Things Not Seen* by Andrew Clements. Penguin Putnam, 2002. 5–6. Average high schooler Bobby wakes up one morning anything but average—he's invisible! His shocked parents insist on secrecy, fearing dangerous reactions. His career mom overcompensates with smothering concern and his scientist dad handles his own fear by theorizing and rationalizing, leaving Bobby to navigate an emotional and physical minefield without much help, until he befriends a pretty blind girl. A real page-turner.

- *The Weather Atlas* by Keith Lye. Running Press, 2001. 4–6. This busy but appealing oversized picture book has it all—from exploring specific weather phenomena to forecasting to global warming. Clear text and great visuals combine to invite and involve the reader. A good starting place for research.

- **Welcome to the Sea of Sand** by Jane Yolen, illustrated by Laura Regan. Putnam, 1996. 2–6. In lyrical language and rich, subtle colors, Yolen and Regan invite us to explore the surprising and complex ecosystem of the Sonora Desert. Look for similar Yolen titles on other ecosystems as well.

- **A Wrinkle in Time** by Madeleine L'Engle. Farrar, Straus and Giroux, 1976. 4–6. In this Newbery Award winning first volume of L'Engle's Time Quartet series, Meg Murry, her brother Charles Wallace and their friend Calvin O'Keefe travel through time and space to rescue Dr. Murry, imprisoned on a dark planet by an evil being whose ambitions for conquest include the earth. L'Engle's masterful blend of fantasy worlds, science fiction, suspense, endearing characters and ethical reflection still scores a hit with young readers as it speculates about the fourth dimension and beyond.

- **Zoo in the Sky: A Book of Animal Constellations** by Jacqueline Mitton, illustrated by Christina Ballit. National Geographic Society, 1998. 2–6. Lilting prose and lush, shimmering illustrations lead us through the night sky to explore more and less familiar animal constellations. Endnotes and star maps add solid science to the magical effect of the book.

Nonprint Resources

There are many educational series, in both print and video formats, that teach science concepts. You are probably aware of popular, highly entertaining programs like The Magic School Bus books and videos or Bill Nye the Science Guy. The videos included below represent series that may be less familiar but deserve consideration.

- **Animal Planet—Sing with the Animals.** Rhino Records, 1998 (CD). 2–4. This delightfully silly collection of songs about animals includes both original recordings like "See You Later, Alligator" by Bill Haley and His Comets and hilarious remakes like "Born to be Wild" by Chickenwolf! You might use it as background music or feature specific songs just for fun.

- **Carmen Sandiego Math Detective: ACME Agent Handbook.** Broderbund Software, Inc., 1998 (Interactive CD). 2–6. Students help crack the case of the missing global landmarks in this engaging, multi-level math game. Rich graphics, clever animation and imaginative sci-fi gizmos entertain while leading students through a series of strategies that practice math skills.

- **Electricity** produced by Andrew Schlessinger and Tracy Mitchell. Library Video Company, 2000 (VHS). 4–6. One of many titles in the Physical Science in Action series, this has an appealing teen host sharing her investigation of the basics of electricity, from subatomic particles to completing a circuit. Demonstrations are clever and effective; the narration is clear and easy to follow. A substantial and palatable introduction.

Web Resources

- **Bay Kids' Weather**
library.thinkquest.org/3805/?tqskip1=1
This ThinkQuest site takes a fun approach to a serious look at weather. Along with a quiz, stories, jokes and myths, the Weather Recipes section explains specific weather phenomena. If you are unable to access the Web address, visit ThinkQuest (www.thinkquest.org) and search the Internet Challenge Library by site title.

- **BrainPop Science and Math**
www.brainpop.com
Interactive movies, time lines, quizzes and other activities on many specific topics within math or science. While this is a subscription site, it allows visitors some preselected free activities each day and a one-time free trial subscription.

- **Education Place Brain Teasers**
www.eduplace.com/math/brain/index.html
Weekly math puzzles at three different grade levels.

- **Math Cats: Fun Math for Kids**
www.mathcats.com
An outstanding, visually appealing site that offers "playful exploration of math concepts."

- **Science Friday Kids' Connection**
www.sciencefriday.com/kids/sfkc-ento.html
This teacher's site offers summaries of NPR's weekly programs along with discussion questions, activities and related resources to use with students.

- **The Yuckiest Site on the Internet**
yucky.kids.discovery.com
Kids will love this exploration of the science of bugs, worms, bodily functions, etc.

Activities for the 500s

Use these activities in the media center or classroom, as parts of a single-period library lesson or in cooperation with classroom teachers. The ideas address standards across the curriculum.

- **Song and Story: Seeing Stars.** Read *Zoo in the Sky* aloud. Then have the class join you in singing "Twinkle, Twinkle Little Star."

- **Dewey 500s Matching Game.** Have students match words related to the DDC 500s to their proper 10s grouping using the Matching Game worksheet on page 71.

- **Felt Board Food Chain Story.** Choose one of the food chains from *Pass the Energy, Please!* "A Chain of Four on the Meadow Floor" or "Woodland Mix Makes a Chain of Six" works well for this activity. Create simple felt figures for each link in the chain, making each character large enough to completely cover its prey. Place the characters in order from right to left on the felt board. As you read the poem, show each animal consuming (covering up) its energy source until only the top of the chain remains visible. Liven up the Woodland Mix, for example, by placing the spider higher so it can "drop" onto the caterpillar and the bird higher yet, so it can "swoop" up the spider. You might also add appropriate habitat props, like grass and trees, for visual interest.

- **Logic Puzzles.** Revisit the logic puzzles activity from the 100s Chapter, using the opportunity to remind students that the same general subject can have several different aspects related to different parts of the DDC. In this case, the word "logic" has a particular application in mathematics, where it refers more to specific standards of objectivity and quantified proof than to general skills of rational and systematic argument.

- **Game: Scientist Charades.** Write the names of 8–16 scientists familiar to your students on slips of paper. Fold the slips and place them in a container. Divide the class into four teams. Review the basic gestures used in charades. If the class is unfamiliar with the game, you might create a chart of basic signals to post in the room. Then have a member of the first team draw a name. Give that student three minutes to prompt his or her team to shout the correct name, using appropriate gestures only. If they identify the scientist within three minutes, record their time and have the next team draw a name. If not, they accumulate three minutes of time and the next team continues to guess the same name. Proceed through all four teams. After several rounds of play, the winning team is the one with the least amount of total time accumulated. **Note:** In choosing scientists to include consider names from this chapter's books, popular scientists like Steve Irwin or Bill Nye, those discussed in your students' classrooms or those presented as part of the extra credit research activity on page 70.

- **Discussion: Challenging Conventional Wisdom.** Review *Starry Messenger.* Discuss the price scientists sometimes pay for questioning the traditional beliefs of their times, using the following prompts. You might carry this further with older students by staging a debate about the value vs. the dangers to society of some new scientific information identified by the class as controversial. A good example might be new discoveries about human DNA and cloning.

  – Why did the Church punish Galileo for sharing his discoveries?

  – Why is new information sometimes frightening to people and to social institutions? Is the discovery of new ideas and information that change the way we look at the world sometimes dangerous? Give examples.

- What other scientists from history were resented, ridiculed or punished for their advanced thinking?

- Do the concerns of traditional thinkers make new scientific discoveries any less true?

- Can you think of any scientists today who struggle against the opposition of traditional thinkers who feel threatened by their work?

- **Visual Arts/Language Arts Tie-in.** Share samples from *Dino Riddles*. Then place the book at a learning center and have students write and illustrate their own riddles about dinosaurs or other animals.

- **Extra Credit Book Reviews.** Invite students to read *A Wrinkle in Time, Things Not Seen, The Number Devil, The Case of the Barfy Birthday* or other fiction titles related to the Dewey 500s, and turn in book reviews that evaluate the books in terms of both their general appeal and their effectiveness at stimulating interest in science or math. Use the reports along with book jackets to create a display in the media center.

- **Dewey-ing the Decimals.** In cooperation with classroom teachers, have older students study decimal numbers to help them locate items identified in the catalog on the shelves. While it's easy to see that 598.1 comes before 598.7, it's harder to grasp why 598.173 precedes 598.2. When students compare Dewey call numbers running out several decimal places, have them fill in the shorter number with zeroes as placeholders. In the example above, they'll compare 598.173 with 598.200. Then let them practice putting either catalog cards representing books, or actual groups of books, in order by decimal numbers.

- **Experiments and Demonstrations.** Coordinate with classroom teachers to divide the class into 10 pairs or small teams; assign each team one of the tens groupings

in the Dewey 500s. Challenge each team to come up with a simple experiment or demonstration related to some aspect of that grouping and present it to the class. *The Ben Franklin Book of Easy & Incredible Experiments, Eco-Fun* and *The Number Devil* are good starting points.

- **Probability and Fairness.** A basic premise of deciding what's fair is giving people an equal chance to succeed. Use the activities at the end of *No Fair!* to explore the mathematical concept of probability as it relates to fairness.

- **Visual Arts Tie-in: Ecosystem Art.** *The Salamander Room* and *Welcome to the Sea of Sand* share lyrical descriptions of ecosystems. Review these books with the class. Then invite students to complete one of these assignments:

- Choose an animal, as in *The Salamander Room*, and draw a picture of the fantasy habitat you might create for it in your room.

- Choose an ecosystem and create a work of visual art that shows the plants, animals and climate that make it up.

- **Dramatic Challenge.** Cast and rehearse the book *Math Curse* as a reader's theater, and perform it for other classes. The story can accommodate many readers. Along with the main character, different students might read the words of Mrs. Fibonacci, Mr. Newton, Russell, Molly, Mom, Dad and each of the multiple choice or extra credit options for each word problem.

- **Extra Credit Research/History Tie-in.** In cooperation with classroom teachers, invite students to use classroom and media center resources to learn all they can about a famous mathematician or scientist from the past or present. *Beakman's Book of Dead Guys and Gals of Science* might get them started. Students should complete the biography worksheet on page 72 to share their findings.

Dewey 500s Matching Game

Draw a line from the subject in the first column to the book spine containing the appropriate Dewey 500s tens group in the second column.

The life cycle of a sunflower

Volcanoes

Science encyclopedia

Food chains on the arctic tundra

Cannibal animals

Newton's laws of motion

Saturn's rings

Matter as solids, liquids and gases

Animals of the Mesozoic period

How to add fractions

Mathematician or Scientist
Biography Worksheet

Research your chosen mathematician or scientist and complete this worksheet. Don't forget to draw or copy and paste an appropriate picture in the center to represent your subject or his/her work.

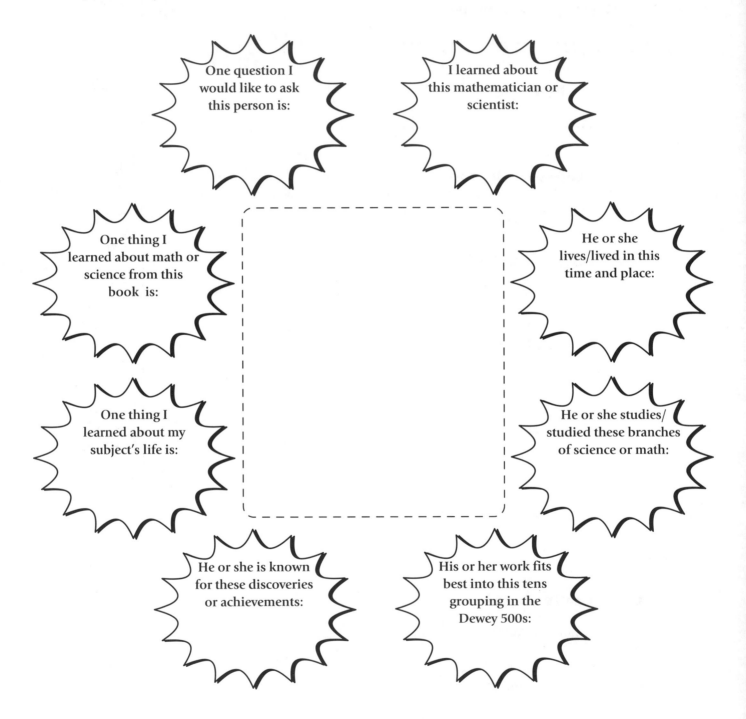

One question I would like to ask this person is:

I learned about this mathematician or scientist:

One thing I learned about math or science from this book is:

He or she lives/lived in this time and place:

One thing I learned about my subject's life is:

He or she studies/studied these branches of science or math:

He or she is known for these discoveries or achievements:

His or her work fits best into this tens grouping in the Dewey 500s:

600s: Technology: Taming & Using the Natural World

Technology, or applied science, is the subject of the Dewey 600s. Like the 300s, this category covers a multitude of ideas—inventions, construction, agriculture, health care and safety, family life and cooking, pets, robots, transportation and communications technology and more. And while we may think of science as objective and impersonal, applied science touches the core of human nature as it explores how we restless, inventive humans bend and shape nature's forces and resources to solve problems and improve our lives.

Also like the 300s, many subjects in the 600s overlap with other hundreds categories. While wild horses are covered in the 500s, their domestic cousins belong here. The line between architecture, found with the arts in 720, and engineering and construction, which fit here, can be hazy. And what exactly distinguishes business (650s) from commerce (380s)? If your students haven't discovered it already, now is the time to make sure they understand that organizing all of human knowledge is not an exact

science. Sometimes Dewey simply had to assign subjects as best he could. That's why we use subject headings and cross references in our library catalogs, just as we use key words to search the Internet.

An interesting teacher resource book is *Inventors and Inventions: Creative Cross-Curricular Activities, Fascinating Background Information, Problem-Solving Investigations* by Lorraine Hopping Egan (Scholastic, 1997). It offers ideas and resources about inventing. Along with activities that address curriculum standards in social studies, math, science, language arts and visual arts, it includes a foldout board for "The Great All-Time Inventions Game."

Congratulations! You and your little brother finally figured out a way to solve the space problem in your room. Bunk beds! Your parents agreed to design and build them so they'll be strong, safe and a perfect fit. But you complained so much before you found a solution that they're making you work together to pay for the building materials. So you're reading up on moneymaking ideas for kids. You're taking a babysit-

ting class, hoping to get jobs watching neighbor children. And you might start a dog walking business as a service to busy pet owners on your block. Your Mom is so impressed with how well you're cooperating that she's promised to make your favorite meal to celebrate when you've earned the money! Now you're worried that you'll be so busy you'll need a robot to clean your room and do your other household chores ... All these ideas—designing and building bunk beds, starting and managing businesses, babysitting, pet care, cooking, robots—and many more are covered in the Dewey 600s, which are all about using natural forces and resources, combined with creativity, to solve problems and make things to improve our lives.

These are the tens groups in the 600s category:

- 600s: General Works about Technology
- 610s: Medicine and Health
- 620s: Engineering
- 630s: Agriculture
- 640s: Home Economics and Family Living
- 650s: Business Management
- 660s: Chemical Engineering
- 670s: Manufacturing
- 680s: Manufacturing for Specific Purposes
- 690s: Building and Construction

Here are some print and nonprint resources related to technology. They, along with other titles from your collection, could be placed on display or built into your lesson plans.

Print Resources

- ***Because of Winn-Dixie*** by Kate DiCamillo. Candlewick Press, 2000. 3–6. This highly acclaimed novel is an instant classic in the "kid and her dog" genre, and much more. Opal moves to a small southern town, where her loneliness for her old friends, mysteriously absent mother and emotionally distant father draw her to a big, ugly, lovable dog. The two befriend a cast of local eccentrics in a gentle, heartwarming story of community, sadness, humor and hope. "Magical realism" at its best.

- ***The Beloved Dearly*** by Doug Cooney. Simon & Schuster, 2002. 3–6. Ernie is a born entrepreneur. In this funny and surprisingly sweet story, he assembles an odd assortment of misfits to join his bizarre business of staging pet funerals in a vacant lot. He's all about the money until his own dog dies and he discovers that he's provided a real service and gained real friends.

- ***Brainboy and the Deathmaster*** by Tor Seidler. HarperCollins, 2003. 4–6. Despite the hokey title, Seidler delivers a fast-paced, high tech, science fiction thriller that pits a group of brainy orphans against a revered, but secretly evil, millionaire who is using the captive kids to help him defeat aging and death. Aspects of computer technology, chemical and genetic engineering earn this title its place here.

- ***Cook-A-Doodle-Doo!*** by Susan Stevens Crummel, illustrated by Janet Stevens. Harcourt Brace, 1999. K–4. In this bright, lively takeoff on the tale of the Little Red Hen, Big Brown Rooster and his barnyard friends (including turtle and iguana!) create a delicious treat, with unexpected results.

- ***Cows, Cats and Kids: A Veterinarian's Family at Work*** by Jean L. S. Patrick, illustrated by Alvis Upitis. Boyds Mills Press, 2003. 2–5. Mike Patrick is the only veterinarian for a small rural community in South Dakota. In this book, his wife shares the family's life and the work in a way that defines it for parents and kids alike. Chapters in the voices of each child, combined with crisp, evocative photos, draw readers into the story.

- ***Feather, Flaps, & Flops: Fabulous Early Fliers*** by Bo Zaunders, illustrated by Roxie Munro. Penguin Putnam, 2001. 2–5. Learn about the "dynamic personalities and trail-blazing exploits" of seven heroes and heroines of aviation, including "Wrong Way" Corrigan and Bessie Coleman. The light-hearted text and big, vibrant illustrations honor the courage and creativity of these early flyers.

- ***Great Building Stories of the Past*** by Peter Kent. Oxford University Press, 2002. 4–6. Early on Kent observes, "…people learned that if they worked together, if they used their ingenuity, with simple tools, patience and hard work they could change the world—and they did." That pretty much sums up the Dewey 600s! The book celebrates Herculean feats of architecture and engineering like the Great Wall of China, the Eiffel Tower and the Panama Canal, using detailed illustrations, unusual angles and fascinating text to convey the sheer magnitude of these accomplishments. Exceptional.

- ***I Love Planes!*** by Philemon Sturges, illustrated by Shari Halpern. HarperCollins, 2003. K–3. Bright, bold illustrations and loosely rhyming text characterize this picture book celebration of all kinds of aircraft and spacecraft.

- **Mistakes that Worked** by Charlotte Foltz Jones. Doubleday, 1991. 4–5. The hallmark of inventors is perseverance, and it sometimes produces surprising results. This book tells about many well-known inventions that came about as mistakes, while their inventors were pursuing other goals.

- **More Homer Price** by Robert McCloskey. Scholastic, 1999. 3–5. Aside from some dated language (e.g., "dames"), these clever, warm, familiar stories of Homer and Centerburg, Ohio, hold up very well. This collection features a famous plant breeder whose legacy is seeds for super-sized ragweed, a shyster who sells the invisible and mysterious Eversomuch More-So, and the grave (and hilarious) dangers of jukeboxes.

- **Mrs. Rose's Garden** by Elaine Greenstein. Simon & Schuster, 1996. K–3. Mrs. Rose yearns to win a blue ribbon at the fair for her vegetables. But when it looks like she's found the secret and will win them all she realizes it would be more fun to share the wealth, and secretly transplants from her garden to those of her friends.

- **Native American Medicine** by Nancy Bonvillain. Chelsea House, 1997. 5–6. This Indians of North America series title conveys various Native attitudes and approaches to health and illness, healing and healers and the role of spirituality in healing from the distant past to the present. Handsome and informative.

- **Oh, the Things You Can Do that Are Good for You! All About Staying Healthy** by Tish Rabe, illustrated by Aristides Ruiz. Random House, 2001. K–3. In wacky, wonderful Dr. Seuss style, this Cat in the Hat's Learning Library title introduces basic health care concepts like exercise, cleanliness, nutrition, rest, dental care and safety. The discussion of sneezes is, as you can imagine, especially enlightening! Colorful, lighthearted and right on target.

- **Pretend Soup and Other Real Recipes: A Cookbook for Preschoolers and Up** by Mollie Katzen and Anne Henderson. Ten Speed Press, 1994. K–3. The authors offer fun recipes with both written and pictorial directions. Designed for preschoolers and up, the recipes are simple enough for classroom use. Kid reviews, cooking hints and safety tips add to the fun.

- **Ricky Ricotta's Mighty Robot vs. the Mecha-monkeys from Mars** by Dav Pilkey, illustrated by Martin Ontiveros. Blue Sky Press, 2002. 2–4. Pilkey and Ontiveros's Ricky Ricotta books are light, cartoon-style romps through silly, "save the world" adventures. This one is no exception. Along with the robot action are fun features that have students drawing the characters and flipping pages to create an animation-like effect.

- **The Rusty, Trusty Tractor** by Joy Cowley. Boyds Mills Press, 1999. K–3. Despite pressure from the local salesman, Granpappy trusts another season to his vintage tractor. This warm celebration of down-home country values and humor is perfect for reading aloud, and might inspire you to create a display of farm equipment and related books from your 600s collection.

- **So You Want to Be an Inventor?** by Judith St. George, illustrated by David Small. Penguin Group, 2002. 2–6. St. George and Small score a solid hit with this humorous look at the history of inventing and inventors. Their amusing, irreverent treatment doesn't imply a frivolous approach to the subject; the information is well researched and intriguing. A sneakily informative riot of a picture book that sends a clear "Go for it!" message.

- **Wingwalker** by Rosemary Wells, illustrated by Brian Selznick. Hyperion Books for Children, 2002. 2–6. This lovely, sensitive story traces the changes in an Oklahoma boy's life during the Depression, when his family must leave their small farming community. Reuben's courage is tested by his father's new job as a daredevil wingwalker for a group of traveling fair performers. Large print and straightforward, engaging text make this a good transition piece from readers to chapter books; aspects of agriculture and aviation in the story give it a place in this category.

Nonprint Resources

- ***The Magic Schoolbus Goes to Seed*** directed by Larry Jacobs and Charles E. Bastien. Scholastic, 2003 (VHS). K–4. Ms. Frizzle takes her class on another wild adventure, in search of a plant for the class garden. Their ladybug school bus provides an up close and personal look at the parts of a flower, tying in both botany from the 500s and agriculture.

- ***The New Way Things Work*** by David Macaulay. DK Interactive Learning, 1998 (interactive CD). 2–6. This visually appealing, easy-to-use software version of Macaulay's award-winning book offers easy access to rich information on many aspects of technology. Great for individual exploration or review of key concepts.

- ***This is a Hospital, Not a Zoo!*** by Roberta Karim, narrated by John McDonough. Recorded Books, Inc., 1998 (audiocassette). K–3. Young hospital patient Filbert McFee tries to evade unpleasant medical procedures and the formidable Nurse Beluga by turning himself into a series of animals. A whimsical, witty story that will resonate with children.

Web Resources

- **BBC Kids' Health**
  www.bbc.co.uk/health/kids
  This site offers a "body tour" along with information and games related to physical and mental health.

- **Challenger Learning Center**
  www.challenger.org
  Find the location of the nearest Challenger Learning Center and teacher resources related to spacecraft.

- **FDA Kids' Home Page**
  www.fda.gov/oc/opacom/kids
  A colorful site that features food safety and various medical treatments.

- **PetStation: The Guide to Enlightened Pet-Keeping**
  www.petstation.com
  This site offers information on companion animals and their care.

Activities for the 600s

- **Story and Song.** Read aloud *Mrs. Rose's Garden* to younger students. Follow up by singing the words below to the tune of "Down by the Station." To add a visual element, make large, bright vegetables for use with a felt board to prompt each new verse of the song.

  Out in the garden,
  Early in the morning,
  See the _____ _____ all in a row.

  Here we go to pick them,
  Then we will eat them.
  Pick, pick, eat, eat.
  Off we go.

  (Fill in the two blanks with desired vegetables and colors, like this: See the red tomatoes all in a row.)

- **Discussion: Inventors and Inventing.** Introduce *So You Want to Be an Inventor?* Then use these prompts to discuss the process of inventing.

  - What is the difference between discovery and invention? (Start with a good children's dictionary. *Inventors and Inventions,* mentioned on page 73, addresses this question.)

  - Name some things that people have discovered; name some things that people have invented.

  - Why do people invent things?

  - What kind of person invents things? What qualities do the inventors in *So You Want to Be an Inventor?* have in common? (List qualities like curiosity, perseverance, creativity, etc., on the board.)

  - Have you ever invented anything? (Point out that new recipes, new designs for paper airplanes or new ways to organize things are all inventions—Melvil Dewey was definitely an inventor!)

  - What would you like to invent? What problem would you like to solve with a new idea, tool, machine or system?

- **Technology Acrostic Puzzle.** Have students practice creativity and show what they know using the worksheet on page 81. Depending on ages and skill levels in your class, this puzzle can be used in different ways. You might simply write it on the board, read it aloud and talk about both the acrostic form and what the poem has to do with technology. You might review the sample and create an acrostic as a class. Or you might assign individual students to create individual compositions, using the handout.

- **Game: What Invention Am I?** Use this fun, "get-moving" game to consolidate learning about inventions as the fruit of technology. Tape a sign with the name of a different popular invention on each student's back. Skim this chapter's books for ideas of buildings, machines, foods, systems, etc., to include. Then let students circulate, trying to identify what they are by asking yes/no questions. The first one to three students to correctly identify their signs are the winners and may receive small prizes. Let the game continue until all students have guessed correctly, helping as needed.

- **Creative Expression: Dramatic Readings.** This chapter's books contain lots of drama and humor. Assign each student to find a favorite brief selection from one of the books to read to the class as expressively as possible. The goal is to make fellow students appreciate the drama or the humor of the passage. Look for humorous passages in *More Homer Price* or *Oh, the Things You Can Do that Are Good for You!,* or for dramatic passages, turn to *Wingwalker* or *Because of Winn-Dixie.*

- **Creative Challenge: Applying Science.** Build on your reading and the discussion and games by challenging students to come up with inventions of their own. Have them start by thinking about problems they'd like to solve. How could they make a new-and-improved hot fudge sundae? A faster skateboard? Safer playground equipment? Once they have problems to tackle, have them brainstorm ideas for solving them, and develop at least one idea into plans, an outline, drawings or a model of a solution they've invented. Have fun with this! Allow wildly creative, "science fiction" inventions, as well as practical ideas. Conduct a Show-and-Tell event, or even a mini-Inventors' Fair, to share their results. Have students vote for their favorite inventions and award ribbons in different categories like Most Practical Invention, Most Creative, Most Helpful Invention, etc. You might create an award for each tens group of the Dewey 600s.

- **Kitchen Creations: Cooking!** Borrow a kitchen in the school and prepare favorite recipes to share. You might start by reading *Cook-A-Doodle-Doo!* aloud and then use the recipe in the book to make strawberry short-cake. Or try a recipe from *Pretend Soup and Other Real Recipes.* As you cook, talk about how recipes and cooking are examples of applied science.

- **Math/Research Tie-in: Calculate the Savings. (**Note: You will need to make one larger copy of each chart shown on the worksheet on page 82.) Many inventions are designed to save people time. Divide the class into teams of four to five students. Assign each team one of these inventions: microwave oven, washing machine, cell phone, digital camera, power lawn mower, copy machine. Give each team one enlarged copy of the appropriate chart. The teams will estimate the time needed to complete the tasks listed on their chart and calculate the time saved by newer methods or

machines. "Best guesses" based on research, interviews with older people or common sense are acceptable for use in these calculations. After each team has completed its chart, compile the teams' work for everyone to see, using a completed and enlarged or overhead transparency version of the worksheet. For an added challenge, have students calculate their charted times in minutes, or make up word problems, based on the completed tables, for students to solve.

- **Visual Arts/Language Arts Tie-in: Poems in Celebration of Technology.** Introduce *I Love Planes!* Then place it at a learning center and challenge students to create their own illustrated, poetic celebrations of inventions or products of technology that make their lives better. Results can be presented to the class or used in a display in the classroom or media center.

- **Challenger Learning Centers.** After the *Challenger* space shuttle disaster in 1986, the Challenger Center for Space Science Education was formed to honor the lost crew. The organization provides first-rate educational experiences through Challenger Learning Centers, found in science museums in about 30 U.S. cities. These amazing centers include rooms which simulate a space capsule and mission control, and allow students to experience, firsthand, the tasks and stresses of an astronaut or mission controller. Is there one near you? Visit the Challenger Learning Center Web site to find the closest centers. Not only can students visit these centers in field trip mode, but they can also participate in simulated missions, with advance preparation. If there is no center near you, take advantage of the online resources to provide exciting space education experiences in the classroom.

- **Booktalks.** Assign students to read *Because of Winn-Dixie, The Beloved Dearly, Wingwalker, Brainboy and the Deathmaster, Ricky Ricotta's Mighty Robot vs. the Mechamonkeys from Mars* or *More Homer Price.*

Students will prepare brief (one to two minute) talks for the class, designed to entice others to read their book. Booktalks are similar to oral book reports, but less analytical and more entertaining. They often end with a cliff-hanger. For a fun follow-up activity, poll the class to see who plans to read which book, based on which booktalk.

- **History Tie-in: Group Research.** Assign older students one of the tens groups from the Dewey 600s. Prepare by studying your media center collection, and weighting the number of students assigned each tens group according to its representation in the library. If your local collection's 660s (Chemical Technology) section is sparse, you might only assign it to one student. Try to include each tens group if possible.

Students' tasks will be to browse that specific part of the collection, find information about one specific issue or invention within it and note the dates of 1–3 important developments in its history. For example, Chapter 2 of *Mistakes that Worked* explains that by 400 BC people were using tea made from willow bark to relieve pain. In 1853 a Frenchman mixed another chemical with salicylic acid from willow bark to improve the remedy, and in 1894 a German rediscovered the aspirin we now use. Once students have completed their research, compile results to produce a time line of interesting developments in human technology.

Technology Acrostic Puzzle

An acrostic puzzle is a word puzzle that can be read both up and down, and across.
The letters of a word or name, written up and down, are used in other words or
phrases written from left to right, to create a meaningful composition.

First look at this example:

We u **S** e

s **C** ience to

I mprove our

liv **E** s

a **N** d solve

diffi **C** ult

probl **E** ms

Now, using the word "inventions," provided below, write your own acrostic composition.

I
N
V
E
N
T
I
O
N
S

Calculate the Savings

Method or Machine	Time to cook dinner (macaroni and cheese)
Open fire	
Kitchen stove/oven	
Microwave oven	

Method or Machine	Time to cut the lawn
Hand scythe	
Manual mower	
Power mower	

Method or Machine	Time to wash and dry one large load
By hand, tubs and clothesline	
Wringer washer and clothesline	
Modern washer and dryer	

Method or Machine	Time to notify family in another town of an emergency
Letter by post	
Telegraph	
Cell phone	

Method or Machine	Time to send relatives in another town picture of new baby
Portrait artist	
Early glass plate camera	
Digital camera	

Method or Machine	Time to make 25 one-page copies from an original
Handwritten	
Early printing press	
Photocopy machine	

700s: Fine Arts & Recreation: "Playing" with Talent and Creativity

How do you use your leisure time? Do you watch or play sports? Do craft projects or play games? Go to movies or concerts? Visit art galleries or attend plays? Or maybe you work in one of the sports or performing arts that provide these enriching experiences, and appreciate the talent, creativity and discipline involved. Few of us will become rich and famous as artists, dancers, actors, musicians or sports stars. But the potential for self-expression, growth and simple satisfaction of participating as dabblers or dedicated amateurs is enormous. These pursuits, for both participants and spectators, are the subject of the Dewey 700s. Along with the obvious—art, dance, drama, music and well-known sports—you'll find martial arts, cartoons, architecture, postage stamps, photography, crafts, table games, word puzzles and brain teasers.

Remember when we first started talking about the Dewey Decimal classification system? You were late for a soccer game and couldn't find your uniform because your room was a mess. As you learned about grouping and organizing subjects in the DDC, you used similar ideas to organize your room so you could find things more easily. Now your soccer uniform is stored in your closet and your equipment on a shelf—you'll never be late to a game again! What else is on that shelf? Your baseball glove? Ice skates? Your trumpet and music for school band? The Magnificent Magic Kit you share with your brother? Your easel and paints? The wood burning set you got for your birthday? Where are your favorite music CDs and movies? Do you have so many that you need to arrange them by type or by title? All of these extracurricular activities—music, drama, art, crafts, sports—fall into Dewey's 700s category, called Fine Arts and Recreation.

Here are the tens groups in the 700s category:

- 700s: General Works about Arts and Recreation
- 710s: Civic and Landscape Art
- 720s: Architecture
- 730s: Sculpture and Plastic Arts
- 740s: Drawing, Decorative Arts and Crafts
- 750s: Painting and Paintings
- 760s: Graphic Arts (Printmaking, postage stamps)
- 770s: Photography
- 780s: Music
- 790s: Recreation and Performing Arts

The following resources, along with other titles from your collection, could be placed on display or built into your lesson plans.

Print Resources

- ***Annabelle the Actress Starring in Hound of the Barkervilles*** by Ellen Conford. Simon & Schuster, 2003. 2–3. Annabelle is serious about her acting, so she's thrilled to get a role in a local play. But how will she handle her huge, slobbering doggie costar and the evil intentions of her nemesis, Lowell Boxer? A fun title for young readers transitioning to chapter books.

- ***Arches to Zigzags: An Architecture ABC*** by Michael J. Crosbie, illustrated by Steve and Kit Rosenthal. H. N. Abrams, 2000. 2–6. This alphabet picture book uses striking photos to illustrate architectural elements. A four-line poem for each element encourages readers to look at form and function in creative ways. Endnotes offer further explanation and identify the buildings pictured.

- ***The Baby Grand, the Moon in July, and Me*** by Joyce Annette Barnes. Penguin Putnam, 1998. 3–6. Annie Armstrong dreams of being an astronaut like Neil Armstrong, who is about to walk on the moon. But during the historic days of *Apollo 11*, Annie has a mission of her own—to reconcile her family, split over her brother's dream to be a jazz pianist. Likable Annie's gumption will delight readers.

- ***Beethoven Lives Upstairs*** by Barbara Nichol. Scholastic, 1994. 3–5. In Vienna in 1822, Christoph writes letters to his uncle complaining of the chaos caused by the family's new renter, Ludwig van Beethoven. Over time, Christoph comes to understand the lonely, eccentric genius and to care for him. The letters weave actual incidents from Beethoven's life with fictional characters and events.

- ***A Caldecott Celebration: Six Artists and their Paths to the Caldecott Medal*** by Leonard S. Marcus. Walker & Co., 1998. 2–6. This appealingly designed book uses photos, quips and quotes, sketches and finished illustrations and lively narration to provide intimate glimpses of extraordinary artists, whose work spans the six decades of the Caldecott Medal. Marcus's choice of vignettes will delight children and help them see the artists as "real people."

- ***Jackie & Me*** by Dan Gutman. HarperCollins, 2000. 3–5. In this time travel adventure Joe Stoshak travels to 1947 to research a class assignment about Jackie Robinson. He is startled to find that he's been transformed into a black boy, and shares in Robinson's experiences of racism during the baseball great's rookie season. Lots of sports action keeps the reader riveted as memorable lessons about the evils of prejudice and the triumph of human dignity emerge.

- ***Kids at Work: Lewis Hine and the Crusade against Child Labor*** by Russell Freedman. Clarion Books, 1994. 5–6. Freedman tells the story of Lewis Hine, teacher-turned-photographer who dedicated himself to educating people about the evils of child labor through his photos. Freedman's readable, sincere text teams up with Hine's photos to create an impact that should help twenty-first century children appreciate the legacy of Hine's work in their own lives.

- ***King of Shadows*** by Susan Cooper. Simon & Schuster, 1999. 4–6. Eleven-year-old Nat, who has suffered trauma and grief, lives for acting. He's thrilled to join a troupe and travel to England to perform Shakespeare's plays at The Globe Theatre. But Nat finds more adventure than he bargained for, as he is pulled back in time to perform with the Bard himself. Cooper weaves her magic in this exciting character and period novel.

- **_Lives of the Athletes: Thrills, Spills (and What the Neighbors Thought)_** by Kathleen Krull, illustrated by Kathryn Hewitt. Harcourt Brace, 1997. 3–6. This fun collective biography introduces 20 remarkable twentieth century athletes, covering a wide range of sports and a diverse group of sports greats, including Hawaiian surfer Duke Kahanamoku and Chinese martial arts guru Bruce Lee. The tone is informative and gossipy; clever illustrations accent the eccentricities of the subjects. Use it in chapters like a picture book or as a starting point for research. Sister volumes called _Lives of the Artists_ and _Lives of the Musicians_ are also useful. These titles are available as talking books.

- **_"Now I Get It!" 12 Ten-Minute Classroom Drama Skits for Science, Math, Language, and Social Studies, Volume II: Grades 4–6_** by L. E. McCullough. Smith and Kraus, 2000. 4–6. This teacher's resource book includes skits designed to consolidate learning in the title subjects through drama. Simple skits with stage direction, prop suggestions and pre- and post-play activities offer a fun change of pace.

- **_One Smooth Move_** by Matt Christopher. Little, Brown and Company, 2004. 2–3. Count on Christopher for play-by-play action to entice young sports enthusiasts to read. This easy transitional title offers lots of skateboarding action in a plot with mystery elements and new-kid drama. Slight, but useful in representing non-team sports for young readers.

- **_Rain or Shine Activity Book: Fun Things to Make and Do_** by Joanna Cole and Stephanie Calmenson, illustrated by Alan Tiegreen. Morrow Junior Books, 1997. 2–6. This easy-to-follow guide features humorous black-and-white cartoon style drawings and instructions for nearly 100 games, riddles and craft projects. Activities are grouped in chapters like "Card Games," "Paper Crafts" and "Brainteasers."

- **_Savion: My Life in Tap_** by Savion Glover and Bruce Weber. William Morrow & Co., 2000. 4–6. Glover's enthusiasm leaps off the pages of this vibrant, colorful book full of history, action and street slang. Weber highlights Glover's prodigious talents as dancer and choreographer (_Bring in 'da Noise, Bring in 'da Funk_). Chapters in Glover's voice focus on his training, heroes and determination to "give back."

- **_The Secret of the Great Houdini_** by Robert Burleigh, illustrated by Leonid Gore. Simon & Schuster, 2002. 2–6. Gently sketched characters and intense colors and textures combine with immediate, present tense text to draw the reader into the thrilling suspense of a child watching a gripping Houdini escape. An endnote adds context, but the story stands alone as a powerful picture book experience.

- **_Shooting Star: Annie Oakley, the Legend_** by Debbie Dadey, illustrations by Scott Goto. Walker & Co., 1997. 2–6. You'll be "tickled to jelly" with this tall-tale version of real events in the life of the "greatest sharp-shooter in the universe." Clever, lush illustrations make you love Annie whether she's creating Pike's Peak and the Hawaiian Islands, or "jawing with royalty."

- **_Surviving the Applewhites_** by Stephanie S. Tolan. HarperCollins, 2003. 5–6. Thirteen-year-old Jake has one last chance to make good, after being kicked out of numerous schools. He finds himself in the Creative Academy home school run by the artsy, eccentric and narcissistic Applewhite family. There Jake is accepted without fuss, adopted by an odiferous dog and a loquacious pre-schooler and left to find his own way in the creative chaos around him. The passionate and riotously dysfunctional Applewhites work their careless magic and help Jake find his gifts and his place in the world. Edgy, funny and poignant.

- **_Tallchief: America's Prima Ballerina_** by Maria Tallchief with Rosemary Wells, illustrated by Gary Kelley. Viking, 1999. 2–6. In this beautiful book, Tallchief tells of being "born with music that flowed through my body as naturally as blood in my veins," and her need to express that music in dance. Her loving, supportive family life and wealthy background as daughter of an Osage father and Scots-Irish mother challenges stereotypes. Satisfying and broadening.

Nonprint Resources

- ***Beethoven Violin Concerto, Bernstein Serenade*** performed by Hilary Hahn. Sony, 1999 (CD). 2–6. Youthful prodigy Hahn was in her teens when she made this recording, but started studying violin at age four and debuted with the Baltimore Symphony Orchestra at nine. Use this as background or for quiet listening, drawing attention to the discipline required for a young musician to make it in the competitive world of classical music.

- ***National Gallery Complete Illustrated Catalogue on CD-ROM: Expanded Edition*** by the National Gallery. Yale University Press, 2001 (Interactive CD). 4–6. This software lets students explore the riches of the National Gallery's collection of thirteenth through twentieth century works by Western European masters. Graphics are superb and the program easy to use. Students can browse or research in Artists' Lives, Historical Atlas, Picture Types, General Reference and Guided Tours—all nicely cross-linked.

- ***The Trumpet of the Swan*** read by the author, E. B. White. Bantam, 1978 (audiocassettes). 2–5. Louis is a trumpeter swan born without a voice, who compensates by learning to play the trumpet! He finds joy in the music, but is determined to restore his family's honor before pursuing his own goals, which include winning the heart of his beloved Serena. A classic.

- ***Wonderfulness*** by Bill Cosby. Warner Brothers, 1998 (CD). 2–6. This re-release of Cosby's 1960s comedy recording holds up well and will delight students with Cosby's irresistible brand of wacky, wholesome wit that always rings true.

Web Resources

- **Cartoon Critters**
  www.cartooncritters.com
  A fun learn-to-draw site that also features puzzles, games, jokes and riddles.

- **Dance-Kids**
  www.dance-kids.org
  Information on different kinds of dance all over the world, including a photo gallery, stories and games for younger students.

- **Humor: Our Sixth Sense**
  library.thinkquest.org
  Choose "Libraries," "Internet Challenge Library," then key word search by site name.

- **MysteryNet's Kid Mysteries—Magic Tricks**
  kids.mysterynet.com/magic

- **NGA Kids**
  www.nga.gov/kids/kids.htm
  A bright, fun site offering information about items in the National Gallery's collection, an animated story and interactive art projects.

- **Sports Illustrated for Kids**
  www.sikids.com/index.html

Note: Many arts organizations, sports associations, athletes and performers have official Web sites; nearly every sport has a Hall of Fame site. Search the name of an individual, sport or organization to find them.

- **Book Discussions: What Do Sports and the Arts Mean to Us?** Use this chapter's titles and/or others from your collection to explore the role that sports and the arts play in our lives. Have students choose a sport or art form that interests them and read a related picture book or fiction title. Try to use multiple books about each subject so you have at least two books represented in each discussion. For example, students interested in drama might read a mix of these titles: *Annabelle the Actress Starring in Hound of the Barkervilles, King of Shadows, Surviving the Applewhites.* After students read their books, gather them by subject to talk about what their sport or artistic discipline means to the characters in the books—what they learn from participating and why it's important to them. Then invite students to talk about sports or arts activities that are meaningful to them and why. After the small group discussions, have the whole class share ideas about the role of sports and the arts in general.

- **Discussion: Athletes and Entertainers as Social Activists.** People in sports and the arts sometimes use their skills to try to right wrongs or improve conditions in society. Have half of your fifth or sixth grade students read *Jackie & Me* and the other half read *Kids at Work: Lewis Hine and the Crusade against Child Labor.* Then use these prompts to discuss participants in sports or the arts as social activists.

  - What was Jackie Robinson's talent? What problem in society did he address by using his talent?

  - What was Lewis Hine's talent? What problem in society did he address by using his talent?

  - What challenges did each man encounter as he tried to use his skills to make life better? What dangers did each face because he chose to stand up for justice?

  - How successful was each man at solving the problem or making things better? How is our country better today because of what each man did?

  - What other artists or athletes have used their talents and fame to try to make life better for others? Explain who they are and what they do.

  - If you became famous for your talent, what social issues would you like to address and how would you go about making things better?

- **Arts and Recreation Letter Tiles.** Have students learn vocabulary related to the Dewey 700s using the worksheet on page 91. **Answers:**
  STA*TUE, sculpture
  TEL*LER OF JO*KES, comedian
  MAR*TIA*L A*RT, karate
  CRE*ATI*NG DAN*CES, choreography
  CON*TES*T, tournament
  DES*IGN*ING BU*ILD*ING*S, architecture
  SER*IOU*S O*R T*RAD*ITI*ONA*L, classical

- **Story and Action Poem.** Read aloud *Shooting Star* or *Tallchief* to younger students. Then act out this poem about enjoying the arts and recreational activities.

  I can really pitch and swing,
  (*Make pitching and batting motions.*)
  And you should hear me when I sing!
  (*Fan out hands below mouth.*)
  My pictures decorate the wall,
  (*Use thumb and first finger of each hand to define corners of a picture frame.*)
  And I can kick a soccer ball.
  (*Wind up and kick.*)
  I like to fish, play checkers, too,
  (*"Cast" a line, jump checker across an imaginary board.*)
  And I can dance the old "soft shoe."
  (*Shuffle feet as if tap dancing.*)

I'm handy with a hot glue gun, *(Use hand to make shooting motion, blow on barrel.)*
I'm very good at having fun! *(Make a silly face and jiggle fingers and hands.)*
I'll make a rabbit disappear—
(Wave pretend magic wand.)
I'm talented! It's very clear. *(Take a bow!)*
But after all is done and said, I close my eyes, and fall in bed! *(Make hands into a pillow under cheek and close eyes.)*

- **Games: Don't Just Stand There, Play Something!** Introduce *Rain or Shine Activity Book* or another book of game rules found in the 790s. Then set out cards, board games and other appropriate materials and let students play in small groups, referring to the rules as necessary.

- **Game: Entertainment Bingo.** Use the handout on page 92 to play this game. Adjust the time investment and challenge level by assigning it to individuals or teams, or by requiring students to complete either one vertical, horizontal or diagonal row or the entire sheet to win. Give students a limited amount of time with appropriate reference or 700s resources to find answers. The first student or team to correctly complete the required squares is the winner. All answers can be found in this chapter's books; most should be available in any basic reference collection.
  Answers:
  H, AO, RM, BL
  BD, HH, SG, WS
  MS, LVB, BC, JR
  LH, MT, DK, CVA

- **Applied Science: Entertaining Snacks.** What snacks do students enjoy while they watch TV, movies or sports events? Brainstorm, create a snack menu and prepare the snacks together to enjoy while you watch an appropriate video presentation— perhaps a clip from *Wonderfulness.*

- **Math and Science Tie-ins: The Play's the Thing.** Work with classroom teachers to incorporate drama into grades 4–6 math or science lessons. Use the scripts and instructions in *"Now I Get It!"* to explore the metric system or fractions, bird flight, magnets or sources of energy.

- **Language Arts: Fan Letters.** Have students write to their favorite living athletes, musicians, visual or performing artists, explaining why they chose that person and inviting a response. Mail the letters (look for addresses on the Internet or send in care of an associated organization) and see who writes back! While e-mail might be quicker, you could take this opportunity to practice the vanishing art of the handwritten letter.

- **Creative Expression: Arts & Recreation Mobiles.**
  Collect materials and have students create works of kinetic sculpture (mobiles) featuring symbols of their favorite sports, arts, games or other Dewey 700s activities.

  Materials needed:

  - sturdy paper plates (1 per student)

  - assorted construction paper, card stock or heavy solid-colored wrapping paper

  - crayons and felt-tip markers

  - scissors

  - colored yarn

  - tape or stapler

  Directions:

  1. Color/decorate the paper plates.

  2. Draw a spiral on each paper plate from an edge to the center and cut along the line, forming a coil.

  3. Attach a length of yarn to the center of the paper plate (now the top of the coil) using staples or tape. This is how you will hang the mobile.

4. Cut shapes representing artistic or recreational activities (sports equipment, musical instruments, etc.) from assorted papers. Students may write brief statements about what the activities mean to them on both sides of the symbols.

5. Cut three or more lengths of yarn, then attach one or more symbols to each piece of yarn with staples or tape. The shapes should hang down in interesting formations from the coil.

6. Attach the lengths of yarn to the coil with staples or tape so that they form an attractive, balanced mobile.

- **Creative Expression: Arts & Recreation Collages.** Provide poster board, old magazines, scissors, glue, crayons, markers and access to computer clip art if possible. Have students create collages of words and images that represent the history and stars of their favorite arts, sports or recreational pursuits. Display collages in the media center or classroom and discuss the images.

- **Research/Creative Expression: Mining Classroom Talent.** Each student will choose an athlete, sportsman, game master, architect, musician or other performing artist who shares an interest or talent with the student. For example, a would-be pro-

fessional basketball player might choose Tim Duncan; an aspiring magician might select Harry Houdini. After choosing, students will research independently to complete the three phases of the assignment. *Lives of the Athletes: Thrills, Spills (and What the Neighbors Thought)* and *A Caldecott Celebration: Six Artists and Their Paths to the Caldecott Medal* are good places to start.

- Learn about the person's life and write a one-page biography.

- Review the person's creative work and summarize it for the class using visuals, recordings, etc., as appropriate.

- Prepare and present their own creative expression, based on the interest they share with the artist. A young musician researching Clara Schumann might perform part of one of her compositions for the class. A fan of Bill Cosby might deliver part of one of his comedy routines.

Encourage creativity! Let costumes and theatrics be part of this celebration of talent.

- **Field Trip: Architecture Walk.** After reading *Arches to Zigzags: An Architecture ABC*, go for a walk around your school's neighborhood. See how many of the architectural elements defined in the book you can find.

Arts and Recreation Letter Tiles

Rearrange the letter tiles to form definitions for the words below, which all relate to subjects covered in the Dewey 700s. Then write the word below each tile set. The number of words in each definition is given in parentheses. An example is done for you.

architecture (2) **choreography (2)** **classical (3)**

comedian (3) **karate (2)** **popular (3)**

sculpture (1) **tournament (1)**

Example:

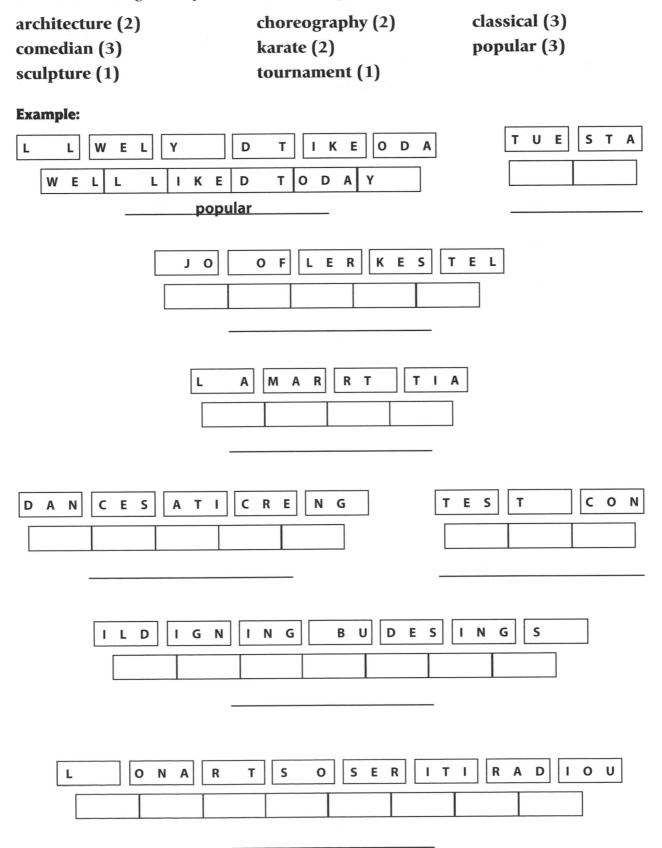

L	L	W E L	Y	D	T	I K E	O D A

W E L L	L	I K E	D	T	O D A	Y

_____ **popular** _____

T U E	S T A

J O	O F	L E R	K E S	T E L

_____

L	A	M A R	R T	T I A

_____

D A N	C E S	A T I	C R E	N G

_____

T E S	T	C O N

_____

I L D	I G N	I N G	B U	D E S	I N G	S

_____

L	O N A	R T S	O	S E R	I T I	R A D	I O U

_____

Entertainment Bingo

Use classroom or media center resources to identify athletes or performers in the bingo squares below. Indicate your answer by writing the initials of the appropriate entertainer across the square in colored marker or crayon.

Maria Tallchief (MT)   **Savion Glover (SG)**   **Duke Kahanamoku (DK)**

Robert McCloskey (RM)   **Harry Houdini (H)**   **Chris Van Allsburg (CVA)**

Bill Cosby (BC)   **Annie Oakley (AO)**   **Babe Didrikson (BD)**

Ludwig von Beethoven (LVB)   **Hilary Hahn (HH)**   **Maurice Sendak (MS)**

Jackie Robinson (JR)   **Bruce Lee (BL)**   **Lewis Hine (LH)**

William Shakespeare (WS)

Daring escape artist	Famous sharp shooter	Kept ducks in his studio to help him illustrate a story	Martial arts and movie star
Top female athlete of the first half of the twentieth century	Child prodigy pianist	Created and performed in *Bring in 'da Noise, Bring in 'da Funk*	Late sixteenth to early seventeenth century British stage actor (better known as poet and playwright)
Won Caldecott Award for *Where the Wild Things Are*	Classical composer best known for his Ninth Symphony	African American actor, author and comedian	First black athlete to play major league baseball in U.S.
Used photographs to fight against child labor in U.S.	Native American prima ballerina	King of Hawaiian surfing	Wrote and illustrated book (*Jumanji*) that was made into a movie

800s: Literature: Communicating in Writing

Literature in its many forms is the subject of the Dewey 800s. Included are prose, poetry and plays and their interpretation and criticism; the creative, professional and technical aspects of authorship; and the arts of letter writing, speech and debate. The word "literature" can refer to the entire body of written work related to a particular language, culture or subject. Or it can be reserved for selected examples from a body of work that are considered to be of excellent quality or universal interest.

As with the study of languages in the 400s, the scope is well-defined. But the limitations noted in the 400s, regarding the ethnocentricity of concentrating on Western literatures and tossing everything "else" into the last catch-all tens group, carries over into this category. In fact, Dewey transplants the geographic/linguistic arrangement of the 400s directly, as you'll see in the list below. From a modern perspective, it might seem more useful to break literature down by forms or processes rather than linguistic regions. But there it is—Dewey made

decisions that made sense in his time and place, from his perspective. We use and adapt it as best we can. As with the 400s, confronting this limitation head-on with students offers opportunities to look at changing, increasingly global attitudes towards the world's languages and cultures, and the literature they produce.

Another tricky aspect of the 800s is determining what belongs in the non-English language tens groups. Most libraries place their collections of works in foreign or multiple languages in the 430s–490s. So what does that leave for the 830s–890s? It's a bit elusive, and libraries may handle it differently. In general, libraries place translations and analyses or study guides of well-known literature from non-English languages (e.g., *The Odyssey*) in the 800s, and lighter works that might be used to learn a language (e.g., picture books with text in English and Spanish) in the 400s.

Precocious students might ask why we don't put all storybooks—picture books, chapter books, the whole world of children's fiction—in the

800s. The answer is that, using the broader definition of literature, we could. But most libraries and media centers recognize that this isn't the best practical arrangement. Readers use fiction differently than nonfiction. Separating out the fiction for easy browsing just works better. As with many aspects of using the DDC, these decisions require judgment and practical thinking about how a particular library's patrons use the collection. Compilations of classic children's stories, for example, might be found in the fiction stacks, in the 390s with folklore or in the 810s or 820s as English language literature. It's not an exact science! We need to rely on library catalogs to point us in the direction that reflects local decisions. This is a good time to introduce (if you haven't already) or reinforce the distinction between fiction and nonfiction. Remember the easy, if superficial, trick from the "Do We" Really Know Dewey? Web site mentioned in the introduction to this book? You can "only say 'NO' once: Fiction=Not true, Nonfiction=True."

You're not speaking to your little brother. He snooped through your things and found your journal, in which you write notes and poems about your private thoughts and feelings. Now he's teasing you and threatening to tell your friends about the things that upset you, or even spill the beans to the new kid in your class whom you have a little crush on. You're furious! So far, you've kept him quiet by threatening to throw his collection of fantasy books in the trash. But how long will that last? Why did you write those

things down in the first place? You never meant for anyone to read them. And, for that matter, why does your brother care so much about his silly wizard and dragon books? The human, creative urge to express ourselves and our feelings in written words, the need to share information and our desire to reach beyond our limited lives or to find ourselves in the thoughts, feelings and experiences of others recorded in writing, are what literature, and the Dewey 800s, are all about.

These are the tens groups in the 800s category:

- 800s: General Works about Literature
- 810s: American and Canadian Literature
- 820s: English Literature
- 830s: German Literature
- 840s: French Literature
- 850s: Italian Literature
- 860s: Spanish & Portuguese Literatures
- 870s: Latin Literature
- 880s: Greek Literature
- 890s: Literatures of Other Languages

Resources on the 800s

Here are some resources to help you discover the Dewey 800s. They, along with other titles from your collection, could be placed on display or built into lesson plans. **Note:** Upstart, a division of Highsmith, has an attractive poster series featuring four kinds of poetry: limerick, couplet, acrostic and haiku. The bright, appealing posters give examples and instructions for writing these special poems, and could be used to stimulate a creative writing exercise or anchor a display.

Print Resources

- ***And the Dish Ran Away with the Spoon*** by Janet Stevens and Susan Stevens Crummel. Harcourt, 2001. 2–3. We all know the famous nursery rhyme. It's recited every day. But that's the problem, because **this** time, after they ran away, the Dish and the Spoon didn't come back! The rhyme can't go on without them, so the cat, dog and cow search the land of nursery tales to find the runaways. Lots of fun in an oversized picture book.

- ***The Better Brown Stories*** by Allan Ahlberg. Viking, 1996. 3–6. Unhappy with the boring stories The Writer has thought up for them, the Brown family demands more exciting ones. But be careful what you wish for! This highly original premise, full of British humor, rollicking action and delicious irony, explores the strange and wonderful relationships between a writer and the characters he creates.

- ***The Color of My Words*** by Lynn Joseph. HarperCollins, 2000. 3–6. Ana Rosa is only 12, but she's a writer, which is a dangerous thing for even a child to be in the repressive and politically corrupt Dominican Republic. This intensely personal, lyrical story unfolds through a combination of narrative and Ana Rosa's poems, and paints a picture of both family strength and the social dysfunction that surrounds Ana Rosa and wreaks havoc with her life.

- ***Cool Melons—Turn to Frogs! The Life and Poems of Issa,*** story and translations by Matthew Gollub, illustrated by Kazuko G. Stone, calligraphy by Keiko Smith. Lee & Low Books, 1998. 2–6. This creative team brings to life the expressive charm of haiku through a lush combination of text about the life of Japanese poet Issa, calligraphic renderings and translations of his poems, and illustrations that showcase his fascination with the natural world.

- ***Dateline: Troy*** by Paul Fleischman. Candlewick Press, 1996. 5–6. In accessible two-page spreads, Fleischman deftly weaves narrative retelling of excerpts from *The Iliad* with newspaper headlines and clippings from the 1950s–90s. The dramatic juxtapositions emphasize the timelessness of this ancient classic and the universality of the human characteristics it expresses.

- ***David v. God*** by Mary E. Pearson. Harcourt, 2000. 5–6. When David and his high school biology classmates die in a car accident during a field trip, David knows it's a mistake. He can't be dead! David, who has always gotten by on charm and bravado, challenges God to a debate to win his return to Earth. While preparing for the debate with his classmate Marie, brainy "Queen of the Nerds," David begins to learn important lessons about himself, promises and what's really important. Fun, surprising and satisfying.

- ***Lives of the Writers: Comedies, Tragedies (and What the Neighbors Thought)*** by Kathleen Krull, illustrated by Kathryn Hewitt. Harcourt Brace, 1994. 3–6. This fun book introduces 16 exceptional writers from the tenth through twentieth centuries. It covers the standards—Jane Austen, Charles Dickens, Shakespeare—as well as less familiar authors like Murasaki Shikibu and Zora Neale Hurston. Gossipy text combines with Hewitt's delightful, perceptive illustrations to present flesh and blood people with lives full of victory, tragedy and eccentricity. Use it in chapters like a picture book or as a starting point for research.

- ***Look at My Book: How Kids Can Write & Illustrate Terrific Books*** by Loreen Leedy. Holiday House, 2004. 2–4. Leedy offers kids bright, appealing and detailed instructions for producing their own books, step by step, from getting the initial idea to binding the finished product. She offers enough options to stimulate creative thinking without overwhelming kids.

- ***Martin's Big Words: The Life of Dr. Martin Luther King, Jr.*** by Doreen Rappaport, illustrated by Bryan Collier. Hyperion Books for Children, 2001. 2–6. This breathtaking picture book is as beautifully designed and narrated as it is illustrated. Collier's collages, full of symbolic images, and Rappaport's text, interweaving direct quotes from Dr. King, provide a fresh, rich introduction to this hero of the American civil rights movement, who was also a formidable speaker. A Coretta Scott King Honor Book.

- ***Marty Frye, Private Eye*** by Janet Tashjian. Henry Holt & Company, 1998. 2–3. Marty Frye, rhyming junior detective with the heart of a poet, solves three mysteries in his school and neighborhood. A fun, easy chapter book for transitional readers.

- ***So, You Wanna Be a Writer? How to Write, Get Published, and Maybe Even Make it Big!*** by Vicki Hambleton and Cathleen Greenwood. Beyond Words Publishing, 2001. 4–6. This neat, well-organized "how to" title intersperses profiles of real kid writers with clear, manageable directions for everything from finding your genre to overcoming writer's block to submitting work for publication. A good balance of practicality and encouragement.

- ***Three Pigs, One Wolf, and Seven Magic Shapes*** by Grace Maccarone, illustrated by David Neuhaus. Scholastic, 1997. 1–2. This Hello Math Reader series title cleverly builds on the classic children's story, "The Three Little Pigs," to create a new story that introduces geometric shapes. By using a tangram in a variety of ways to support the story, Maccarone encourages children to identify the basic shapes, which together make up a square, and view them in different configurations to make other shapes and puzzles. A pattern and endnotes offer more opportunities to explore shapes, angles and creative possibilities.

- ***Touch the Poem*** by Arnold Adoff, illustrated by Lisa Desimini. Scholastic, 2000. 2–6. This pairing of simple poems that revel in the sense of touch with mixed media collages that reinforce the words and suggest other sensory experiences provides a joyfully familiar celebration of simple pleasures.

- ***The Tree is Older than You Are: A Bilingual Gathering of Poems & Stories from Mexico with Paintings by Mexican Artists*** selected by Naomi Shihab Nye. Simon & Schuster, 1995. 3–6. In this lovely collection you'll find folktales, soulful reflections, sassy little poems and haunting images, all in side-by-side Spanish and English text. Evocative and compelling, it's a great ambassador for both the special flavor of Mexican cultural expression and international sharing.

- ***What Do Authors Do?*** by Eileen Christelow. Houghton Mifflin, 1995. 2–4. This clever, cartoon style introduction to the creative process of writing, with head nods to publishing and marketing as well, demystifies the process for children and encourages them to look for story ideas in their own everyday lives.

- ***When I Was Your Age: Original Stories about Growing Up*** edited by Amy Ehrlich. Candlewick Press, 1996. 4–6. In terms of studying the 800s, this short story collection has 2-for-1 appeal. The stories come from the childhood memories of highly regarded children's authors like Laurence Yep, Katherine Paterson and Avi, so they explore the inspirations and craft of authorship. And they are excellent stories that speak of universal human experiences, exemplifying the narrower definition of "literature." Volume II of the same title, with works by Joseph Bruchac, Jane Yolen and others, is equally good.

- **William Shakespeare & the Globe** by Aliki. HarperCollins, 2000. 3–6. Presented in scenes like a play, with glorious illustrations rich in period detail and lots of tantalizing mini-quotations, this innovative picture book draws the reader into Shakespeare's Elizabethan England. The concept and design are unusual and engaging, and may inspire readers to sample the Bard's work itself. A delightful, award-winning book.

Nonprint Resources

- **Great Speeches of the Twentieth Century.** Rhino Records, 1995 (CD Boxed Set). 4–6. This collection of speeches, including many presidential addresses in their original voices, might be sampled for inspiration or serious study of the art of speech-making.

- **Olive's Ocean** by Kevin Henkes, narrated by Blair Brown. HarperCollins, 2004 (CD Set). 4–6. Before Martha's family leaves to visit her grandmother on the coast, the mother of a classmate who recently died gives Martha a note from the dead girl's journal praising Martha's kindness and hoping for friendship. But the two hardly knew each other. Aside from the facts that they both aspired to be writers and Olive longed to see the ocean that Martha, too, loves, what connects them? Henkes's sensitive insights and spare, eloquent style create a hauntingly lovely coming-of-age story in which writing is an important vehicle for processing emotions. Newbery Honor Book.

- **Shakespeare's Greatest Hits Volume 1** retold by Bruce Coville. Full Cast Audio, 2003 (audiocassette). 3–6. This audio adaptation of Coville's clever retellings of Shakespeare plays, including *A Midsummer Night's Dream, Macbeth, Romeo and Juliet* and *Twelfth Night,* is enthusiastically performed by a cast of actors. Coville blends his own brilliant prose summaries with Shakespeare's words, conveying much of the drama, charm and complexity of the plays for newcomers to the Bard's magic. The books might be used with the tapes; they are beautifully illustrated by Tim Raglan.

Web Resources

- **BrainPop English**
  www.brainpop.com
  Interactive movies, time lines, quizzes and other activities on types of writing and public speaking. While this is a subscription site, it allows visitors some preselected free activities each day and a one-time free trial subscription.

- **Kidscribe**
  brightinvisiblegreen.com/kidscribe
  A fun bilingual site that features poetry, short stories, essays and jokes written by kids. Students are invited to submit their work in Spanish or English.

- **KidsReads.com**
  www.kidsreads.com
  Book reviews, substantial author profiles, guidelines for student book clubs, word games based on popular books and more.

Use these activities in the media center or classroom, as parts of a single-period library lesson or in cooperation with classroom teachers. The ideas address standards across the curriculum.

- **Felt Board Story.** Make cutouts of each nursery rhyme character in *And the Dish Ran Away with the Spoon*. Invite students to prompt you to place each character on the board as it turns up in the story. Then begin reading aloud and demonstrate by putting up the cat, cow and dog from the title rhyme, who appear early in the book. There's lots of room for drama and rhythm in reading this story, and many characters from different rhymes and stories to spot and enjoy. For more elaborate visuals, add a version of the map the animals follow in their search, and arrows as they move from one literary character to the next.

- **Quotefall Puzzle: Discover the Hidden Shakespeare Quotation.** Share excerpts from *Shakespeare's Greatest Hits Volume 1*. Then use the puzzle sheet on page 100 to unscramble a familiar quotation from the most famous English language writer of all time. **Note:** If this kind of word puzzle is new to your students, work through the example with them on the board to show how it's done. Have *William Shakespeare & the Globe* available for students to check their work. (The mystery phrase is: "To thine own self be true," from *Hamlet*.)

- **History/Research Opportunity: Famous Authors.** Introduce *Lives of the Writers*. Have students choose one of the writers profiled in the book and use media center resources to learn all they can about their subject. They should produce, from their research, a one-page mini biography, a picture of the author and a short sample of his or her work to share with the class. Before presenting, you might have students who studied the same author combine their work into one presentation, with different students presenting biographical information, showing the picture and reading the author's work aloud.

- **Discussion: Big "L" or Small "l"?** Use a dictionary to discuss with older students the broad meaning of "literature" (think of it with a small "l") as the entire body of written work from a language, culture or subject; and the narrower definition, "Literature" (think of a capital "L") that includes only works that show excellence or have wide appeal based on timeless, universal themes and experiences. Have students suggest books that might fit in the small "l" definition, but not the capital "L" one, and then books that fit the more exclusive definition. Introduce *Dateline: Troy*. Share at least one two-page spread, reading the story and pointing out the related newspaper headlines. Then explore ideas about literature using these prompts:

  - Does the original Greek work, *The Iliad*, from which these stories are taken, qualifies as capital "L" literature? Why or why not?

  - How about the newspaper articles featured in this book? Small "l" or big "L"? Explain.

  - What about the book *Dateline: Troy*? Is it big "L" literature? Why or why not?

  - What do you think this book tells us about what makes good "Literature"? *(Point out universal themes and human emotions from the stories that are reflected in the newspaper clippings. These elements transcend time and geography; we recognize them as relevant to our lives today.)*

- **Essays: Literary Interpretation and Criticism.** Assign older students to read (or listen to) *David v. God*, *The Color of My Words* or *Olive's Ocean*. Students will write essays that both explain what the literary form discussed in the book (writing or debate) means to the main character in the story, and state their critical opinion of the book as literature. Share a few interesting or insightful examples with the class.

- **Creative Expression: Sense the Poems, Part I.** Read excerpts from *Touch the Poem*. Then have students number off from 1 to 4. Number 1 students will write poems to include in an anthology titled See the Poem. Number 2 students will write for Hear the Poem, number 3 students for Taste the Poem and number 4 students for Smell the Poem. When the poems are written, gather students in their numbered groups to illustrate and bind their work, or display student creations on a bulletin board in titled sections, with the original *Touch the Poem* book anchoring the display. For added challenge, encourage students to write their poems in the form of limericks, couplets, haikus or acrostics, as featured in the poetry posters mentioned in the introduction to this chapter.

- **Science Tie-in: Sense the Poems, Part II.** After writing poems that celebrate other senses the way *Touch the Poem* celebrates touch, have students study the science behind their sensory experiences. Cooperate with classroom teachers to explore the anatomy, physiology, chemistry and physics of touch, hearing, taste, smell and speech.

- **Math Tie-in: Magic Shapes.** Work with classroom teachers to use *Three Pigs, One Wolf, and Seven Magic Shapes* in introducing geometry to younger students. Use the pattern and exercises in the back of the book to explore the shapes, angles and creative possibilities of the tangram.

- **Language Arts/Visual Arts Tie-in:** Introduce *Look at My Book: How Kids Can Write & Illustrate Terrific Books*. Then work with visual arts or computer teachers to help students write and illustrate their own books to share and display. Extend this exercise into a service-learning project by arranging for students to share their books in read-aloud programs with younger students.

- **Language Arts: Debate!** Stage a classroom debate, using the modified rules of debate presented on the worksheet on page 101. To enhance the 800s content of the debate, make your debate about whether a particular contemporary book the class has studied qualifies as "big L" literature, using the more exclusive definition (see the Discussion activity on page 98). Students who participate in the debate might involve the rest of the class by polling them for their opinions on the question and their reasons for them, and then use the points mentioned as they make their arguments. You might enlist the help of your school system's debate coach. Be sure to give participating debaters time to prepare together.

- **Creative Writing: What's Your Story?** Introduce *And the Dish Ran Away with the Spoon* or *The Better Brown Stories*. Then have children imagine that they are characters in a story, advising the writer about how they want their stories to change. Students might either write the dialogue between themselves and their writers as skits to be shared in reader's theater mode, or actually write their "better" short stories.

Shakespeare Quotefall Puzzle

Discover the hidden quotation from the most famous English language writer of all time, William Shakespeare. Watch the quote "fall" into place as you form the individual words by transferring letters within each column from above the double line to open squares below the double line. An example is done for you. **Hint:** Start by moving down any letters from the top that can go only one place below. The hidden quotation is found on p. 47 of *William Shakespeare & the Globe*, by Aliki.

Example:

T	W	E	E	S	S	E	E	T
S	H	E		T	W		T	O
=	=	=	=	=	=	=	=	=
S	W	E	E	T	S	=	T	O
T	H	E	=	S	W	E	E	T

Solution: "Sweets to the Sweet" from *Hamlet*

B	E	N	T	H	U	E	F
T	O		T	R	E	L	E
O	W			S	I	N	
=	=	=	=	=	=	=	=
		=					
			=				
		=					=

Solution: _____ from *Hamlet*

Simple Guidelines for Classroom Debate

RESOLVED: That the book _____ qualifies as
Literature due to its excellent quality and timeless
expression of universal human themes and experiences.

Here's a simple procedure for classroom debate:

1. <u>Moderator (Teacher):</u> Introduce resolution. Then call on each speaker in turn to present arguments.

2. <u>First affirmative speaker:</u> Summarize the book's plot and explain how the conflicts and action are important beyond the limits of this particular book. (Maximum 2 minutes.)

3. <u>First negative speaker:</u> Give your own summary of the plot, stressing why it is "nothing special" and does not deserve to be considered "Big L" literature. Try to counter the arguments of the first affirmative speaker. (Maximum 2 minutes.)

4. <u>Second affirmative speaker:</u> Describe the book's main characters and explain why their personalities, emotions and experiences are important expressions of human experience beyond the specific time and place of the book. Try to counter arguments of first negative speaker. (Maximum 3 minutes.)

5. <u>Second negative speaker:</u> Comment on the book's characters and explain why they are not important beyond the context of the book. Try to counter earlier affirmative arguments. (Maximum 3 minutes.)

6. <u>Third affirmative speaker:</u> Explain what you think are the universal or timeless themes or messages of the book, and why they are important. Summarize affirmative arguments and try to counter earlier negative arguments. (Maximum 4 minutes.)

7. <u>Third negative speaker:</u> Comment on the themes or messages of the book, and why they are not timeless, universal or important. Summarize negative arguments and try to counter affirmative arguments. (Maximum 4 minutes.)

8. <u>Moderator (Teacher):</u> Have the class vote to determine which team, affirmative or negative, made the most convincing arguments.

© 2005 by Diane Findlay (UpstartBooks)

900s: History & Geography: Exploring Where We Live and Where We've Been

In the final hundreds group, Dewey looks back on all we know about the earth, its history and our history on it. He explores the planet in the geography section, then looks at personal histories through biography. He repeats his pattern of taking a geographical approach in the last half of the category. This time, Dewey moderates the ethnocentricity in the system by assigning a tens group to each major continent. The range of the 900s is vast and includes travel, atlases, maps, explorers, archaeology, genealogy and flags of the world along with every aspect of "our story" from prehistory to the present.

In general, the 900s include comprehensive examinations of the changing lives of peoples and nations. Titles that tell very particular stories, like the history of tennis or of health care in America, are almost always placed in the hundreds category that addresses their particular subject. So you'd find the history of tennis in

the 790s, and of health care in the 610s. There is some overlap with the 300s, in which anthropology considers the development of human society over time, and the 500s, which includes geology and paleontology. The handling of biography collections varies from library to library. Be sure to point out where and how to look for biographies in your media center. Often, general collective biographies are shelved in the 920s, but collective biographies about people who share a talent or interest are found with the particular subject matter (e.g., profiles of tennis stars in the 790s, of famous physicians in the 610s), and individual biographies are in a separate section with call numbers reflecting "B" for biography and the last name of the person the book is about.

You're working on a school assignment. You have to interview your grandparents about what life was like when they were your age. You thought it would be boring, but you're surprised. Your grandma shows you a family tree, put together by her mother and kept up by your grandma and your mom, with your name on it! It traces your family back to the 1700s. You never knew you had a pirate among your ancestors, or a famous artist. Your grandma also shows you an autobiography written by her great-great uncle, who came to America from China in the 1800s. He worked building railroads and lived in a Gold Rush town. This is pretty exciting stuff! You never thought before about how you came from a whole bunch of people who lived in different places and had exciting lives. Your grandpa says you got your athletic ability from his family and your dark eyes from your grandma's. And when you tell them about your brother reading your journal, they say maybe you'll take after your however-many-greats uncle and be a writer! You've decided to read up on China, and maybe Scotland, where your dad's family came from. Maybe you'll even travel there someday! But your first stop will be the library. And now, thanks to Melvil Dewey, you'll know just how to go about exploring the 900s and finding the information you need!

There are many publishers' series that deal with aspects of history and geography. Here are some examples:

- Battles of World War II from Lucent Books

- Kidding Around Travel Series from John Muir Publications

- Lives of Notable Asian Americans from Chelsea House

- My America and Dear America historical fiction titles from Scholastic

- Visual Geography from Lerner Publishing Group

- World History from Lucent Books

These are the tens groups in the 900s category:

- 900s: General Works about History and Geography

- 910s: Geography and Travel

- 920s: Biography, Genealogy

- 930s: Ancient History

- 940s: History of Europe

- 950s: History of Asia

- 960s: History of Africa

- 970s: History of North America

- 980s: History of South America

- 990s: History of Other Areas

Resources on the 900s

Here are some resources to use in exploring the Dewey 900s. They, along with other titles from your collection, could be placed on display or built into lesson plans.

Print Resources

- ***The Ballad of the Pirate Queens*** by Jane Yolen, illustrated by David Shannon. Harcourt Brace, 1998. 2–6. Yolen's compelling and sometimes lyrical verse begs us to read aloud the rollicking tale of Anne Bonney and Mary Reade, infamous female pirates of the high seas. There is subtle, ironic humor in the rich formality of the paintings which may be lost on young students. But Yolen's telling of a good story should have wide appeal.

- ***Biography Today: Profiles of People of Interest to Young Readers*** edited by Cherie D. Abbey. Omnigraphics, April 2004. 4–6. Each issue of this slick, substantial serial features about ten 15–20 page profiles of people in the public eye, including politicians, entertainers, athletes and social activists. The design, which punctuates chatty text with black-and-white photos, statistics, factoids and sidebar quotations, is appealing and the prose informative.

- ***Climbing Your Family Tree: Online and Off-line Genealogy for Kids*** by Ira Wolfman. Workman Publishing, 2002. 3–6. Readers become "ancestor detectors" using this information-packed paperback. Motivating stories, fun sidebars, charts, worksheets, questionnaires and recommended online and print resources abound, along with advice for searching primary documents, building family trees and keeping family history scrapbooks. The book addresses the situations of adoptees and nontraditional families as well.

- ***Fair Weather*** by Richard Peck. Dial, 2001. 5–6. This sweet, funny, adventure-packed novel is sure to become an American classic. Set at the Chicago World's Columbian Exposition of 1893, it reveals turn-of-the-century wonders as seen through the unsophisticated eyes of the Beckett children and their surprisingly worldly grandfather. Delightful characters, cameo appearances by celebrities of the day and rollicking humor make this pure pleasure. Read it out loud!

- ***Follow the Dream: The Story of Christopher Columbus*** by Peter Sís. Bantam Doubleday Dell, 1996. 2–6. In lovely, richly detailed illustrations that suggest the vastness of Columbus's vision, and simple, straightforward text, Sís tells of Columbus's boyhood dreams of adventure. His courage and determination to discover a trade route from Europe to the Orient by sailing west produced one of history's most compelling and fateful expeditions.

- ***The Gawgon and the Boy*** by Lloyd Alexander. Penguin Putnam, 2001. 5–6. Details of Depression life permeate this witty, wonderful story. David (The Boy) is tutored by his eccentric aunt (The Gawgon) while recovering from illness. She shares an exciting world of books and ideas that spark his interest as school never has. Snippets of historical heroes and legendary drama mix with routine events of daily life to produce wild, amusing, fantasy adventures in his vivid imagination.

- ***The Geography Book: Activities for Exploring, Mapping, and Enjoying Your World*** by Caroline Arnold. John Wiley & Sons, 2001. 3–6. Compasses, longitude and latitude, globes, time zones, map scales and keys and more are covered in the first half of the book, through clear text emphasizing simple, well-illustrated activities. For example, students make globes from balloons, then cut them apart to experience the challenges cartographers face in trying to picture the earth on a flat surface. The last half of the book treats Earth's land masses, water and weather in the same interesting, hands-on way.

- *Hottest, Coldest, Highest, Deepest* by Steve Jenkins. Houghton Mifflin, 2004. 2–3. Jenkins combines dazzling paper collage art with fascinating facts about the earth's geography to entice even reluctant readers. An extraordinary picture book.

- *Kidding Around Atlanta: A Fun-filled, Fact-packed Travel & Activity Book* by Rosanne Knorr. Avalon Travel Publications, 1997. 2–4. This sample from the Kidding Around Travel Series engages kids in planning and enjoying their trip. In black-and-white for easy copying and coloring, it features maps, word puzzles, mazes and other amusements along with information about the city's history and attractions.

- *The Life and Death of Adolf Hitler* by James Cross Giblin. Houghton Mifflin, 2002. 5–6+. Hitler is so infamous that the location of his remains is kept secret, for fear of attracting dangerous protests or feeding Neo-Nazi fervor. Giblin's comprehensive, engrossing biography sheds light on the life of the charismatic, bizarrely gifted, deeply disturbed and rather pathetic man behind one of the most tragic and shameful chapters in world history. A chilling, challenging read.

- *The Mississippi River: A Journey Down the Father of Waters* by Peter Lourie. Boyds Mills Press, 2000. 3–6. In advanced picture book format, Lourie takes us along on his exploration of the Mississippi from source to mouth via canoe, car and bicycle. Interweaving geography with history and river lore, he conveys a personal feel for the awesome, impersonal force of the river in all its splendor.

- *The Moon over Crete* by Jyotsna Sreenivasan. Smooth Stone Press, 1997. 3–5. In this unusual time-travel story Lily is transported to ancient Crete, where she experiences a culture in which women and men work together with mutual respect and equality. The experience helps Lily deal with troubling issues in her everyday life. Endnotes explain the basis of the author's vision of ancient Cretan society.

- *National Geographic World Atlas for Young Explorers.* National Geographic Society, 2003. 4–6. Revised from the earlier award-winning edition, this excellent atlas reflects new place names, statistics, country flags, etc. Beautifully designed and illustrated with colorful photos, it offers a wealth of information in both essay and graphic formats.

- *1,000 Years Ago on Planet Earth* by Sneed B. Collard III, illustrated by Jonathan Hunt. Houghton Mifflin, 1999. 3–5. It's ambitious—profiling entire regional cultures from 1,000 years ago in two-page spreads dominated by art—let alone taking a global look at a time when global thinking was impossible. Inevitably, the results are general and superficial. But that said, Collard and Hunt do an impressive job of blending carefully chosen details, evocative illustration and engaging narration to create an overview of world cultures in very different states of ascendancy and decline than what we see today. A thought-provoking perspective builder.

- *Pearl* by Debby Atwell. Houghton Mifflin, 2001. 2–6. In this charming picture book Pearl looks back from her seventy-fifth wedding anniversary in 1960 on her family's eventful personal experiences with our young country. From her grandfather's encounter with George Washington to her own with Martin Luther King Jr., she dramatizes the startling immediacy of America's history and the enormous changes seen in even one lifetime.

- *The 13th Floor: A Ghost Story* by Sid Fleischman. Bantam Doubleday Dell, 1997. 4–6. Twelve-year-old Buddy and his sister are drawn back three centuries in time to rescue their ancestors from the gallows—one as an accused witch and the other a marauding pirate! Likable, spunky characters carry this cheerful story which provides details about colonial times while taking the reader on a romp through life, liberty and the pursuit of buried treasure.

- ***The Village that Vanished*** by Ann Grifalconi, illustrated by Kadir Nelson. Dial, 2002. 2–6. Breathtaking illustrations in rich, shadowy colors reinforce the frightening but ultimately victorious story of a whole village of Yao people in Africa who carry out a plan to avoid capture by slave traders. A powerful, uplifting book full of courage, magic and hope.

- ***We Were There, Too! Young People in U.S. History*** by Phillip Hoose. Farrar, Straus and Giroux, 2001. 4–6. The roles of nearly 70 young people from our nation's history are traced through photos, quotations and biographical narrative. Chronological chapters place the youth in time. Alongside famous figures like Sacagawea and Bill Gates are many relative unknowns. A handsome, coffee table-style album.

Nonprint Resources

- ***America Rock*** by Bob Dorough and Lynn Ahrens. Rhino Records, 1997 (CD). 2–6. Like the School House Rock! titles used earlier, this fun educational music was written in the 1970s for TV and recently released on CD. While somewhat dated, it still does well what no one else seems to do—introduce concepts through clever, catchy songs. Here, the songs relate to both American history and government.

- ***Isabel: Jewel of Castilla*** adapted from the book by Carolyn Meyer. Scholastic, 2000 (VHS). 3–6. The Royal Diaries books and videos are well-researched examples of historical fiction. This video shows fifteenth-century Spain torn by civil war, treachery and intrigue, in which a young princess grows toward her role as Queen. While the story presents likable and sympathetic Isabel, it alludes to her later role in sponsoring the devastating Spanish Inquisition. Look for other titles in the series.

Web Resources

- **Archaeological Adventure** library.thinkquest.org/3011/home. htm?tqskip1=1 While not visually rich, this site offers a good introduction to archaeology's methods, tools and achievements. Auditory learners can listen to much of the text. If you are unable to access the Web address, visit ThinkQuest (www.thinkquest.org) and search the Internet Challenge Library by site title.

- **Biographical Dictionary** www.s9.com/biography Biographies of varying depth on over 28,000 people "who have shaped the world from ancient times to the present day."

- **The History Channel—Classroom** www.historychannel.com/classroom/ classroom.html Information and links to other resources on a wide range of history topics including Ellis Island, National History Day awards, history projects and more.

- **History in Song** www.fortunecity.com/tinpan/parton/2/ history.html Musical glimpses of U.S. history from the American Revolution to the 1960s.

Activities for the 900s

Use these activities in the media center or classroom, as parts of a single-period library lesson or in cooperation with classroom teachers. The ideas address standards across the curriculum.

- **Stories and Geography.** Share a picture book from the chapter bibliography. *Hottest, Coldest, Highest, Deepest; The Village that Vanished* or *Pearl* are good choices. Locate, in *National Geographic World Atlas for Young Explorers* or on a globe, places which are mentioned in the book.

- **Song.** Sing these words to the tune of "Alouette," adjusting the rhythm slightly to fit. Combine with a story or introduction to the 900s, or use it to introduce the "Who Makes History" discussion below.

  His story, her story, my story, your story,
  Whose stories really make up history?
  Big story, small story, true story, "tall" story,
  Good or bad, sad or glad, Oh …
  His story, her story, my story, your story,
  All of them together make up history!

- **History & Geography Anagrams.** Use the handout on page 112 to play this game.

- **Discussion: Who "Makes History?"** Invite students to think about why some peoples' stories become part of recorded history and some do not. Consider the following ideas. **Note:** This discussion could introduce "Who's Making History Right Now?" on page 110.

  - Who are some of the people you think have been the most important in history so far? Who had the biggest impact on other people?

  - Did the people you named seek fame or prominence? Or were they thrust into "history" by circumstances beyond their control?

  - Why do you think these people are still remembered today?

  - Is "making history" about doing great deeds the world can't ignore? Or is it more a matter of chance—being in the right place at the right time—or leaving behind written records or oral traditions that express common experiences?

- **Game: Biography/Autobiography: Who Am I?** Prepare a set of index cards, one for each student, with a likely title for a biography on one side and the name (or names) of the subject (or possible subjects) on the other. Craft the made-up book titles to give generous clues about the identity of the person or people it's about. For example, you might choose *My Life as President at the Turn of the Millennium*, with Bill Clinton's name on the flip side. Or *The Unauthorized Biography of the Creator of Harry Potter*, with J. K. Rowling on the back. Look for people and titles that will challenge your students without being too difficult. Then have students pick a card, title side up, and try to guess who the biography is about. Also ask students to guess, from the title, whether this book is a biography or autobiography. Obviously, in the examples above, the first sounds like an autobiography, while the second is probably a biography. This game is flexible. Use a card or two for mental refreshers when you need breaks. Set up teams to challenge each other and keep score, awarding points for correct guesses and bonus points for identifying autobiographies. Or, after students catch on to the game, invite them to submit cards to use in future games. Use familiar local figures too, like your school principal or favorite teachers.

- **Visual Arts Tie-in: History Puzzles.** Show books about specific events in history, like *The Ballad of the Pirate Queens* or others from your 900s or fiction collections. Have students choose a historic event that interests them. They will create a picture to illustrate that event. Make the drawings into jigsaw puzzles by backing them on card stock or cardboard and cutting them into appropriately sized pieces for the class. (You can make master patterns for cutting the puzzles or buy them at craft or educational supply stores.) Keep puzzles in separate folders. Return them to the artists and pair students up. Each pair will swap puzzles, put them together and try to guess what historical event is depicted.

- **Creative Expression: History in Verse.** Read aloud *The Ballad of the Pirate Queens.* Then challenge students, as individuals or in teams, to choose an exciting event from history and write the story as a ballad. Share the ballads with the class. You might combine this with the puzzle-making activity above, and bind the resulting ballads and illustration puzzles together.

- **Game: Mapping for Information!** Divide the class into teams of three to four students. Give each team a book from your 900s collection to hide in the media center or around the school for another team to find. Then each team will make a map leading from the starting place (the media center or a specific spot in it) to the book's location. Be sure the book's title appears on the map. Give teams a limited time and let each choose the form, style and scale of its map. Have several books available that show maps of routes within rooms or buildings. Collect the finished maps and redistribute them to other teams, folded or enclosed in envelopes. Say "Go!" and send the teams to search for their books and return to you. Time each team. Then compare experiences and talk about what made each map easy or hard to follow.

- **Math Tie-in: Mapmaking to Scale.** Work with classroom teachers to have students refine the maps they made in Mapping for Information, so that they are accurate to scale. Refer to chapter 8 of *The Geography*

Book, and help students choose an appropriate scale and make the calculations using fractions or percentages and careful measurement.

- **Science Tie-in: The Mississippi River and the Physics of Fluid Motion.** Work with classroom teachers to use *The Mississippi River: A Journey Down the Father of Waters* in an exploration of physics.
You'll need:

  - six large cutting boards or pieces of wood (about 12" x 18")

  - plenty of clay (Play-Doh® works fine) to make models of river channels

  - a sink for demonstrating with water

  - miscellaneous materials mentioned below

    Provide brown and white clay, and food coloring to use in different combinations to show the patterns of motion clearly.

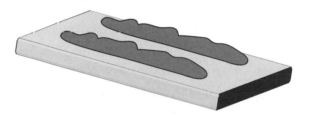

  - Prepare in advance a simple model of a straight river flowing between banks built up with clay on one of the boards.

  - Introduce the book. Explain that rivers are paths for draining rainfall downhill, and that they demonstrate principles of fluid motion as they flow. Rivers might flow in straight lines or loops, fast or slow, calmly or in rapids, depending on the volume of water and the features of land they cross. You will use descriptions from Lourie's book to make models that demonstrate principles of motion.

  - Show your simple model. Hold it over the edge of the sink at an angle, and pour water into the channel from the top to watch it run.

- Divide the class into five teams. Assign each team a passage from the book that describes interesting fluid dynamics of the river. The teams will create models of clay on their boards that show the conditions of the river described in their passages. Encourage them to be creative, using clay, water, food coloring and the angle of the board in the sink to best advantage.

- As each team demonstrates, discuss the influence of gravity, water volume, slope, momentum, friction, etc., on the water and the land it cuts through.

Here are the passages:

- Part One (Headwaters), p. 10, shallow water and 360-degree loops. (Encourage students to use toothpicks, small twigs or other simple materials to create a beaver dam!)

- Part Two (Upper Mississippi), pp. 15–16, locks and dams. (Provide flexible cardboard or plastic to fashion dams.)

- Part Two (Upper Mississippi), p. 26, confluence with the Missouri River. (Use food coloring to show the effect of the muddy, brown Missouri on the comparatively clear or blue Mississippi above the confluence, try a spray hose to add turbulence to the Missouri.)

- Part Three (Lower Mississippi), pp. 30–31, sediment deposits and dredging. (Use sand to show gradual buildup that impedes the channel, clear with a cardboard or plastic "dredge.")

- Part Three (Lower Mississippi), p. 32, Civil War canal. (Model the river, Island Number 10 and canal built to cut off the natural bend and allow Union soldiers to take the Island.) **Note:** You may need a detailed map of Missouri to create an accurate model.

- **Creative Expression: What's Your Story?** The history we look back on today is just a collection of "his stories" and "her stories." So the history we look back on tomorrow will be a collection of "my stories" and "your stories." What story do you want history to tell about you? Imagine that you are celebrating your one hundredth birthday, and write an article you would like your local newspaper to print about your life and accomplishments.

- **Who's Making History Right Now?** Using the reproducible ballots on page 113, have students nominate people they think are making history today—and will be remembered by history tomorrow—in the local community, the U.S. and the world. Remind students that history makers can be "good guys" like Washington or Martin Luther King, or "bad guys" like pirates or Hitler, and can be remembered for having a positive or a negative impact on society. Hand out ballots, then allow a few days to think about nominations. Based on student ballots, announce the "winners" in each category. If possible, invite a local winner to visit the class and talk about the activities for which students selected him or her. If not, have students learn all they can about the person and write a letter from the class expressing appreciation or concern as appropriate.

- **Creative Expression: Designing a Flag.** Show flags from *National Geographic World Atlas for Young Explorers* and talk about the symbolism of the design of the colors and images on some of the flags. Then have students create their own flags—individual flags to represent themselves, or a single flag for the classroom. Have students explain their designs to the class.

- **Genealogy: Real or Imagined.** Introduce *Climbing Your Family Tree.* Explain how the history of a family's growth can be pictured as a tree. Then have students choose one of these tasks:

  - Talk to your parents about your ancestors. Where did they come from, and when?

Are there famous people among them, or people with outstanding stories or accomplishments? If so, learn all you can about one such ancestor and write a true story about him or her to share with the class. Bring a picture, if you can.

- Think about what kind of person you wish were among your ancestors. Do you imagine yourself descended from a great musician or dancer? A brilliant scientist or a powerful queen? Here's your chance! Write a short story about your imagined ancestor to share with the class. Include a portrait showing how you picture him or her.

- **Kidding Around Your Town.** Introduce *Kidding Around Atlanta.* Then make a similar book for your town. Start by discussing what to include. Assign each student a two-page spread like those in *Kidding Around...,* including the appropriate information and a map, puzzle or other activity to go with it. Compile everyone's work and display it in the media center. Then present your travel guide to your public library!

- **Book Clubs.** Assign older students to read *Fair Weather, The Moon over Crete, The 13th Floor* or *The Life and Death of Adolf Hitler.* While reading, each student will write two to three questions, on separate index cards, to generate discussion. Questions should explore something about the book's plot, characters, setting or main ideas. Gather students by book title, and appoint a facilitator for each "club." The facilitator will collect the questions, group them for similar ideas and pose them to the group for brief comments.

History & Geography Anagram

Anagrams are words made up of rearranged letters found in other source words or phrases. See how many words you can make by rearranging the letters in the source phrase below. Start by trying to make words related to the subject matter of the Dewey 900s. There's a sample below to get you started.

HISTORY & GEOGRAPHY

story

Who's Making History Right Now?

Nomination Ballots

Nominate someone in each category who you think is making history today.

☑ Local History Maker

My Nomination: _____

His/her history-making activities:

Why I think his/her story will be remembered:

☑ American History Maker

My Nomination: _____

His/her history-making activities:

Why I think his/her story will be remembered:

☑ Global History Maker

My Nomination: _____

His/her history-making activities:

Why I think his/her story will be remembered:

Review & Assessment Exercises

Use these ideas to help you review and summarize your study of the DDC, and to assess individual comprehension of the system. All activities assume student access to the basic poster outlining the DDC hundreds categories and tens groups. Feel free to use review exercises for assessment or vice versa, or to use activities borrowed or adapted from earlier chapters in either mode. You'll find additional quizzes, word puzzles or worksheets for students to use as practice exercises on these Web sites:

- **Middletown Thrall Library: Do the Dewey!**
  www.thrall.org/dewey/

- **Quia**
  You'll find an interactive concentration game, flash cards and matching game on the DDC on these pages:
  www.quia.com/cc/7265.html
  www.quia.com/jfc/7265.html
  www.quia.com/mc/7265.html

- **"Do We" Really Know Dewey?**
  library.thinkquest.org/5002
  Or do a key word search on ThinkQuest Libraries and enter the site title in the search box.

Exercises for Group or Individual Review

- **DDC Categories Word Search.** You'll find this puzzle, featuring subjects that make up the hundreds groups, on page 118.

- **Mystery of the Lost Lunch Money Puzzle.** Use the worksheet on page 119. **Answer:** The money belongs to Jamaal.

- **What Goes Where? Game.** Gather 10 letter-size envelopes and mount them on a sheet of poster board as pictured, with the open flaps secured and the pockets open. Label them for the hundreds categories and brief category titles—"000s, Generalities," "100s, Philosophy/Psychology," etc. Then make a set of 30 or more index cards, with subjects on them that students might want or need to learn about. They can be either general or specific, as long as they are meaningful and clear to your students. Add pictures to the cards if you wish. Shuffle the cards and give them to students to place in the appropriate pockets on the board. Check their work and discuss with them any errors or questionable choices. This game is very flexible. You can replace or add to the cards as you wish. Students can work individually, in pairs or teams. If you use the game as a team contest, you'll need more cards and you might copy identical card sets on different colored index cards, one set per team. Teams should shuffle their cards, and take turns drawing cards and placing them on the board. You can either remove cards that are incorrectly placed as you go, or go through the sequence, review the cards on each board at the end and then add up team scores, awarding a point for each correctly placed card.

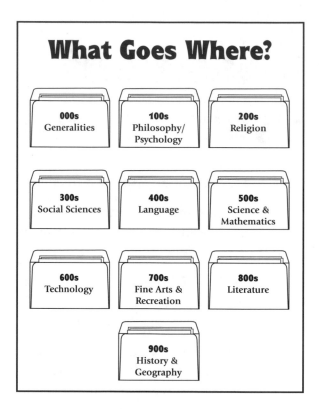

- **Decimal Dynamite Game.** Divide students into teams of about seven to ten players, with equal numbers on each team. (There should be a distance of several feet between teams.) Have each team choose a captain. The players on each team should line up side-to-side. Hand each team member an 8½" x 11" paper with a large printed number containing a decimal, each team having the same set of numbers. (At this point players are only allowed to look at their own papers.) When you say "Go," team players hold up their papers at chest height, numbers facing out, so other players on the same team can see them. The teams

then order themselves according to their numbers, small to large. When the team is in numerical order, the captain raises his or her hand. The first team to accurately order themselves wins.

- **Pirate Treasure Hunt.** Prepare small bags of "loot" containing simple treats—preferably foil-wrapped chocolate coins. You'll need one bag for each team of three to five players to share. Create call number slips for a large variety of books in your collection. Make sure there is only one book in the library for each call number you choose. You'll need four to five slips per team; each team should get a different set of slips. Stash call number slips in the books corresponding to your chosen call numbers, such that each book found will lead students to the next book. Hide a bag of loot for each team behind the final books.

At the beginning of the game, give each team only the first call number slip. When they find their first book, the next call number slip will be tucked inside it, and so forth. The first team to find their loot "rules the seven seas."

To add fun and content to this game, you might provide (or have students make or bring) pirate eye patches, pirate hats or bandanas to wear. You might assign them team names as crew of infamous pirates such as Blackbeard, Anne Bonney, Captain Kidd, etc. And you might start the game with this opening:

Ahoy there, Mateys! Prepare for a treasure hunt! Someone has hidden bundles of treasure in the library stacks, and it's up to you to find the loot. But first, a little about pirates: They have been in existence for about as long as people have been sailing the seas, but about 500 years ago they were a major force in the world when they attacked and stole from explorers bringing home treasures from the New World. Perhaps the most famous of them were Captain Kidd, Black Bart and Blackbeard, who preyed on ships in the 1600s and 1700s. Here's a question. In which

Dewey hundreds group do you think you would find information on pirates? (Answer: 900s, because they are part of history.)

Exercises for Group or Individual Assessment

- **Matching Content to Category.** Use the worksheet on page 120 to assess younger students' grasp of the subject content of the DDC hundreds categories.

- **Fill in the Blank and True/False DDC Review.** You'll find the test and answer key on pages 121–122.

- **Conduct a Simple Search.** Assign individual students, or teams of two to three, a fairly specific subject that they might need to learn about for class, like a country, a person or an animal. Make sure you have titles in your collection that address each assigned subject. Armed with only the word or phrase of their subject, have students go through the process of locating appropriate material in the media center collection. Students will bring their materials to the checkout desk, and explain how they found them either orally or in writing.

- **Why is it There?** Assign older students one of the subject headings below. Their task is to search the catalog for at least two different places where related information appears in the DDC, and explain how the subject fits in each hundreds category and tens group. They will write down their subject and the different Dewey numbers they find. Then, using the DDC chart posted (found on page 126) in the classroom or media center, they will write a short essay explaining their understanding about which aspects of their subject fit in each number. **Note:** You might search these subjects in your catalog in advance, on the chance that you may not have items classed in more than one category, or might use additional

Dewey numbers for aspects of these subjects in your collection.

- Horses (590s, 630s)

- Business (380s, 650s)

- Humor/Jokes/Riddles (390s, 790s, 810s)

- Logic puzzles (510s, 790s)

- Our five senses (150s, 610s)

- Transportation (380s, 620s)

- Communications (380s, 620s, perhaps others)

- **Essay Prompt.** Have students write brief essays addressing these concepts:

- Why do we need the Dewey Decimal classification system? *(To help us organize and find information on any branch of knowledge we want to study.)*

- What are the main organizing principles of the system? *(Grouping like things together, and proceeding from the general to the specific.)*

- What are some of the main hundreds categories in the system and what overall subjects does each include?

- **Multiple Choice Test.** You'll find the reproducible test and answer key on pages 123–125. The test is written in four increasingly difficult skill level sections. Use only as much as is appropriate for your classes. **Note:** Questions in this test are taken from or based on those used in a game called "Dewey Want to be a Millionaire?" found in *Dewey & the Decimals* by Paige Taylor and Kent & Susan Brinkmeyer (UpstartBooks, 2001). You might want to use the game as a review.

Dewey Decimal Classification System Word Search

Can you find the different Dewey categories in the puzzle below?
(Words can go forward, backward, up, down or diagonal.)

```
Y  H  P  A  R  G  O  E  G  J  R  U  Y  T  P
A  R  T  S  A  Y  B  N  R  S  M  H  G  R  I
R  E  C  R  E  A  T  I  O  N  F  T  O  N  Y
F  R  E  Y  E  K  R  W  P  W  O  J  L  G  S
S  E  I  T  I  L  A  R  E  N  E  G  O  E  O
Y  F  N  V  F  G  I  S  Y  L  F  L  H  C  C
P  H  A  O  J  H  Y  T  A  Q  O  L  C  N  I
W  R  P  W  I  R  K  N  E  N  B  D  Y  E  O
Q  D  Z  O  O  G  G  E  H  R  N  X  S  I  L
S  X  J  T  S  U  I  C  F  Q  A  D  P  C  O
K  K  S  I  A  O  E  L  F  Q  O  T  O  S  G
U  I  M  G  N  T  L  P  E  K  Q  D  U  N  Y
H  L  E  H  B  J  J  I  L  R  I  R  C  R  M
R  S  H  U  I  Q  F  U  H  H  H  C  T  N  E
A  Q  H  X  P  I  I  N  L  P  N  L  F  L  R
```

Arts	Literature	Science
Generalities	Philosophy	Sociology
Geography	Psychology	Technology
History	Recreation	
Languages	Religion	

610   507.8
001.942   520   567.9   154.63   787   292.13   808.81   030   385

Mystery of the Lost Lunch Money

Ms. Ortiz took her class to the library for a field trip. While they were there, one of the students dropped his/her lunch money in the nonfiction section in front of the books on European travel. Using the statements and picture below, figure out whose lunch money it is.

- Lauren spent her time in the library looking at books on general information and computers.

- Michiko looked for books on mythology, then went to find some on raccoons.

- Gina thumbed through a book on raising hamsters, then looked through one on building bridges.

- Jamaal picked out some biographies, then walked to the shelves on poetry.

- Nikki got a book on crafts, then another on painting.

- Liza chose a book to read on law, then went to find a Spanish dictionary.

- Mark went straight for the books on basketball, then found a book about jazz.

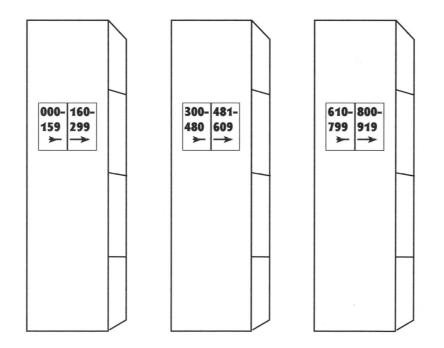

The lunch money belongs to: _____

Hint: If you need help remembering the Dewey Decimal classification ask the librarian to help you locate a chart showing the main classes and subdivisions.

Matching Content to Category

Draw lines connecting the subjects on the left with their Dewey hundreds category on the right.

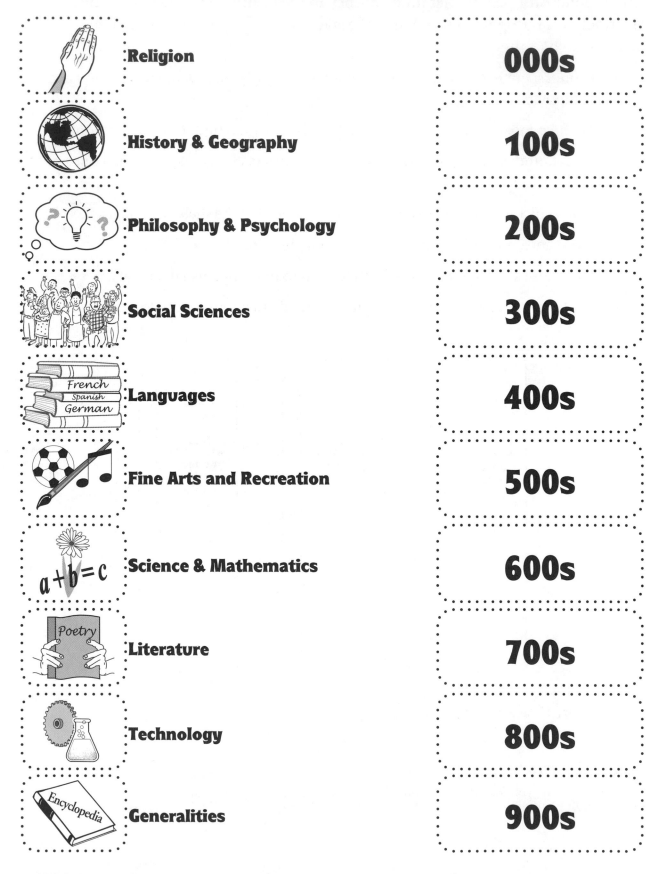

Religion

History & Geography

Philosophy & Psychology

Social Sciences

Languages

Fine Arts and Recreation

Science & Mathematics

Literature

Technology

Generalities

000s

100s

200s

300s

400s

500s

600s

700s

800s

900s

Dewey Decimal Classification Review

Test your knowledge of the Dewey Decimal classification system with this review.

Section I:

Fill in the blanks below.

1. "Biography" is a subject that falls in this hundreds category: (write both hundreds category and tens group).

    _____

2. The first principle of the Dewey Decimal classification system is to group like things _____.

3. The second principle of the Dewey Decimal classification system is to move from the _____ to the specific.

4. Books on drawing and painting would be found in which hundreds category? (Write both hundreds category and tens groups.)

    _____

5. In what tens group of what hundreds category would you find information on playing soccer?

    _____

6. If you wanted to learn about being a librarian, which hundreds category would you search? (Write both hundreds category and tens group.)

    _____

7. You have a new pen pal in Indonesia, and you need to find out where that is. What Dewey number will you look under? (Write both hundreds category and tens group.)

    _____

8. In what hundreds category would you find poetry and plays?

    _____

9. Your aunt is visiting from Mexico. Where will you take her to look for books in Spanish in your library? (Write both hundreds category and tens group.)

    _____

10. Where would you go first if you had to find information on a particular subject in your media center?

    _____

610   507.8   567.9   787   292.13   030   385
001.942   520   154.63   808.81

© 2005 by Diane Findlay (UpstartBooks)

Review & Assessment Digging into Dewey   121

Dewey Decimal Classification Review

Section II:

Circle **T** for True or **F** for False for each of the following statements.

T F 1. The Dewey call number 796.342 is more specific than 796.3.

T F 2. You'll find general titles about technology at the beginning of the 600s rather than at the end.

T F 3. All of the books in your library that tell about horses will be found together in one place on the shelves.

T F 4. The Dewey Decimal system is designed to represent every country of the world equally.

T F 5. Everything written in nonfiction books is absolutely true.

T F 6. Dewey tried to arrange things so that most items on the same subject would be shelved close together.

T F 7. Technology refers to our study of the natural world, unchanged by people.

T F 8. The Dewey Decimal classification system helps us organize and find information in large library collections.

T F 9. Classifying subjects in the Dewey Decimal classification system is an exact science, with no guesswork or overlap.

T F 10. A book of folktales or fairy tales might have a Dewey Decimal number assigned, even though the stories are all made up.

Section III: Extra Challenge

Make up five book titles, and assign them Dewey Decimal classification numbers, choosing the appropriate hundreds category and tens group. Write them on the lines below.

_____

_____

_____

_____

_____

Answer Key

Section I

1. 920s, History & Geography
2. together
3. general
4. 740s and 750s, Fine Arts & Recreation
5. 790s
6. 020s, Generalities
7. 910s
8. 800s, Literature
9. 460s
10. Library catalog

Section II

1. T
2. T
3. F
4. F
5. F
6. T
7. F
8. T
9. F
10. T

Dewey Decimal Classification System Multiple Choice Test

Circle the letter that goes with the correct answer for each of the following questions.

Level 1

1. **The first name of the inventor of the Dewey Decimal classification system was:**

   a. Mervyn

   b. Melvin

   c. Melvil

   d. Malavai

2. **Dewey, the inventor of the Dewey Decimal classification system, was a:**

   a. mathematician

   b. logician

   c. librarian

   d. dentist

3. **When you have tried to find information at the library on your own, but have not been successful, you should:**

   a. ask a librarian

   b. give up and go out for ice cream

   c. call 911

   d. hope someone else in your class found the answer

4. **A call number is:**

   a. the catalog phone number

   b. a prime number

   c. the library's after-hours number

   d. a number on the spine of the book

5. **The computer catalog is the same as:**

   a. the Internet

   b. Web sites

   c. an e-mail system

   d. none of the above

6. **Books on which subject would NOT be shelved next to the others?**

   a. trucks

   b. cartoons

   c. motorcycles

   d. cars

Level 2

1. Books with lots of maps would most likely be found in which section of the library?

   a. 600s

   b. 700s

   c. 800s

   d. 900s

2. Books about the planet Neptune would be found in which section of the library?

   a. 300s

   b. 400s

   c. 500s

   d. 600s

3. In the Dewey Decimal classification system, call numbers range from:

   a. 000–10,000

   b. 000–999

   c. 1–100

   d. 1–10

4. You'd expect to find books on Greek gods and goddesses in what section of the library?

   a. 100s

   b. 200s

   c. 300s

   d. 400s

5. Your first stop when you come to the library to look for information on a particular subject should be:

   a. the catalog

   b. the restroom

   c. the fiction shelves

   d. the information desk

6. Books on which subject would NOT be shelved near the others?

   a. growing corn

   b. dairy farming

   c. ballet

   d. raising chickens

Level 3

1. Books on which subject would NOT be shelved next to the others?

   a. dogs

   b. tigers

   c. lions

   d. elephants

2. At which part of the nonfiction stacks would you look for material on UFOs?

   a. near the beginning

   b. near the middle

   c. near the end

   d. none of the above

3. Books on which subject would NOT be shelved next to the others?

   a. snakes

   b. lizards

   c. iguanas

   d. squirrels

4. A book with a call number in the 920s is probably a:

   a. biography

   b. genealogy book

   c. book of family crests

   d. any of the above

5. An autobiography is a book which:

   a. was printed off the Internet

   b. was written by a person about himself or herself

   c. is about a famous car

   d. none of the above

6. Books on which subject would NOT be shelved near the others?

   a. poetry

   b. advertising

   c. essays

   d. drama

   © 2005 by Diane Findlay (UpstartBooks)

Level 4

1. **Books on which subject would NOT be shelved near the others?**

   a. plays for use in elementary schools

   b. best-loved poems by American poets

   c. classic poems translated from Spanish

   d. classic short stories by American authors

2. **Books on which subject would NOT be shelved near the others?**

   a. philosophy

   b. chemistry

   c. physics

   d. biology

3. **Books on which subject would NOT be shelved near the others?**

   a. fishing

   b. swimming

   c. horseback riding

   d. cooking

4. **Which book would be on the most specific subject?**

   a. 632

   b. 632.245

   c. 632.2

   d. 632–24

5. **A book on public speaking would be found in what area?**

   a. social sciences

   b. technology

   c. literature and rhetoric

   d. the arts

6. **A travel guide for the Middle East would be found in what area?**

   a. generalities

   b. geography and travel

   c. languages

   d. religion

Answer Key:

Level 1

1. c
2. c
3. a
4. d
5. d
6. b

Level 2

1. d
2. c
3. b
4. b
5. a
6. c

Level 3

1. a
2. a
3. d
4. d
5. b
6. b

Level 4

1. c
2. a
3. d
4. b
5. c
6. b

DIGGING INTO DEWEY

000s: Generalities

000s: Unexplained Phenomena, Computers and the Internet
010s: Bibliography
020s: Libraries and Information Science
030s: General Encyclopedias
040s: (Unassigned)
050s: General Interest Magazines
060s: General Organizations and Museums
070s: News Media, Journalism and Publishing
080s: General Collections
090s: Manuscripts and Rare Books

100s: Philosophy & Psychology

100s: General Works about Philosophy and Psychology
110s: Metaphysics
120s: Epistemology, Causation and Humankind
130s: Parapsychology
140s: Philosophical Schools and Doctrines
150s: Psychology
160s: Logic
170s: Ethics
180s: Ancient, Medieval and Eastern Philosophy
190s: Modern Western Philosophy

200s: Religion

200s: General Works about Religion
210s: Natural Theology, Theory of Religion
220s: The Bible
230s: Christian Theology
240s: Christian Moral and Devotional Teachings
250s: Christian Orders & the Local Church
260s: Christian Social Teachings
270s: Christian History
280s: Christian Denominations & Sects
290s: Other Religions of the World

300s: Social Sciences

300s: General Works about Social Sciences
310s: General Statistics
320s: Political Science
330s: Economics
340s: Law
350s: Public Administration, Military Science
360s: Social Problems and Services, Associations
370s: Education
380s: Commerce, Communications and Transportation
390s: Customs, Etiquette and Folklore

400s: Language

400s: General Works about Language
410s: Linguistics
420s: English
430s: Germanic Languages
440s: French
450s: Italian
460s: Spanish & Portuguese
470s: Latin
480s: Greek
490s: Other Languages

500s: Science & Mathematics

500s: General Works about Science and Mathematics
510s: Mathematics
520s: Astronomy
530s: Physics
540s: Chemistry
550s: Earth Sciences
560s: Paleontology
570s: Life Sciences
580s: Botany
590s: Zoology

600s: Technology

600s: General Works about Technology
610s: Medicine and Health
620s: Engineering
630s: Agriculture
640s: Home Economics and Family Living
650s: Business Management
660s: Chemical Engineering
670s: Manufacturing
680s: Manufacturing for Specific Purposes
690s: Building and Construction

700s: Fine Arts & Recreation

700s: General Works about Arts and Recreation
710s: Civic and Landscape Art
720s: Architecture
730s: Sculpture and Plastic Arts
740s: Drawing, Decorative Arts and Crafts
750s: Painting and Paintings
760s: Graphic Arts
770s: Photography
780s: Music
790s: Recreation and Performing Arts

800s: Literature

800s: General Works about Literature
810s: American and Canadian Literature
820s: English Literature
830s: German Literature
840s: French Literature
850s: Italian Literature
860s: Spanish & Portuguese Literatures
870s: Latin Literature
880s: Greek Literature
890s: Literatures of Other Languages

900s: History & Geography

900s: General Works about History and Geography
910s: Geography and Travel
920s: Biography, Genealogy
930s: Ancient History
940s: History of Europe
950s: History of Asia
960s: History of Africa
970s: History of North America
980s: History of South America
990s: History of Other Areas